The New Air Book

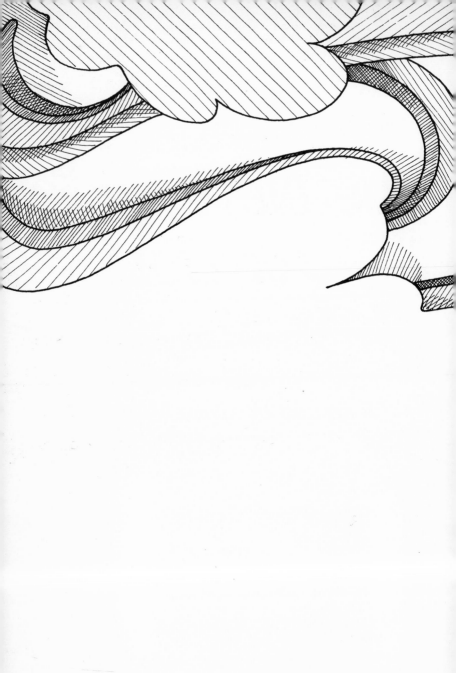

The New
Air Book

MELVIN BERGER
Illustrated by Giulio Maestro

Thomas Y. Crowell Company   New York

Library of Congress Cataloging in Publication Data

Berger, Melvin.
    The new air book.

    SUMMARY: Describes the composition and
characteristics of air, its indispensability to plants and
animals, and the necessity of keeping air fit to
breathe.
    Bibliography: p.
    1. Air—Juv. lit.   2. Air—Experiments—
Juv. lit. [1. Air]   I. Maestro, Giulio, illus.
II. Title.
QC863.5.B47   1974   551.5   74-2355
ISBN 0-690-00444-3

10 9 8 7 6 5 4 3 2 1

BY THE AUTHOR:

Enzymes in Action

Famous Men of Modern Biology

The Funny Side of Science
(WITH J. B. HANDELSMAN)

The New Air Book

The New Water Book

Tools of Modern Biology

For Baba, with love and affection

Contents

The New Air Book

1
Introducing Air

EVERYONE knows about air. It is the gas that completely covers our planet earth. Air is everywhere. In every place where there is no other substance, there is air. And we could not live without a supply of air.

Yet, the more you know about air, the more amazing you find it to be. For example:

• You cannot touch air. Yet air is strong enough to lift objects that weigh many tons.

• You cannot see air. Yet when you look up at the sky, the air above you looks blue.

• You cannot feel air. Yet air is pressing on your body with a weight of over 30,000 pounds.

• The layer of air around the earth goes up about 600 miles. Yet if you go higher than 5 miles in a plane, you must bring along a supply of air or you cannot breathe.

• Fire needs air to burn. Yet when you want to put out a small fire, you blow it out—with air.

• We complain of the hot air in the summer and the cold air in the winter. Yet we would not be able to stand the heat of the sun and the cold of the night for a single day without the protection of the air.

In some ways, air is the most important substance for life. A person might live a month without food, a week without water, but no more than a few minutes without air.

Air is truly amazing. From the very beginning of history, air has fascinated and puzzled man. Slowly we have come to understand air and to learn how to use it. Now we can appreciate the vital part that air plays in the life of man.

2
The Amazing Air

You Cannot See Air, But . . .

Air is real. It is all around us. It fills all the spaces that we sometimes think are empty.

Sometimes we forget that air is everywhere. Then we may say, "The room is empty," or, "There is nothing in the bottle." But the room and the bottle are not empty. They are just not full of anything that we can see. They are full of air.

It is not always easy to realize that air is real. Take a deep breath of air and blow it out through a straw. You cannot see the air coming out. Now hold the straw in a glass of water and blow out again. What happens?

You see bubbles of air form in the water.

Because air is real, it takes up space. Hold a drinking

glass upside down. Push it straight down into a bowl of water. What do you see?

The water fills up only part of the glass. Air fills the rest of the space.

Knowing that air takes space can help you play a trick on your friends. You can show them how you can push a glass with a tissue in it under water without getting the tissue wet.

Crumple a tissue and push it tightly into the bottom of a glass. Press the glass straight down into a bowl of water. Lift the glass and take out the tissue. The tissue will still be dry. The air in the glass kept the water out of the bottom of the glass, where you had the tissue.

Air fills space. Nothing else can be in that space unless the air is pushed out or squeezed into a smaller part of the space.

When you hold a bottle under the tap, the water pushes out the air, and the bottle fills with water. But what happens when you pour water into a bottle so that the air cannot be pushed out?

For this experiment, place a funnel in the neck of a

bottle. Pack some clay tightly around the funnel and the neck of the bottle to make an airtight seal. Pour water into the funnel. Notice how the water drips slowly into the bottle. The clay seal prevents the air in the bottle from getting out. The water can only go in slowly, by squeezing the air in the bottle.

CLAY→

As you do this experiment, the water in the funnel may "burp" as a bubble of air comes to the surface. Can you guess why?

The water is squeezing the air. The air needs more space. Sometimes a bubble of air forces its way through the water in the funnel. The bubble pops when it reaches the top.

To let the water flow more quickly through the funnel, you need to give the air in the bottle a way to escape. You may poke a hole in the clay, or lift the funnel to break the seal. Either way, the water will now fill the bottle more quickly as you pour it.

You Cannot Feel Air, But . . .

Air has weight. Even though you can't feel it, you can prove that air has weight if you have a very sensitive scale.

Place an empty balloon on the scale. Jot down the exact weight of the balloon. Now blow up the balloon and tie the neck. Put the full balloon back on the scale. Write down the exact weight of the air-filled balloon. The difference between the two numbers is the weight of the air in the balloon.

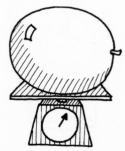

There is a layer, many miles high, of air around our planet earth. This air weighs down on the earth and on everything that is on the earth.

Think of the page of this book that you are now reading, for example. There is a column of air that is the size of this page, and many miles high, pressing down on the page. Although a little air does not weigh much, this column of air is very heavy.

Scientists have found that air has a weight of about 15 pounds on every square inch of surface. The page of this book has a surface of about 45 square inches. That means that air weighs down on this page with a pressure of about 675 pounds. On a large sheet of newspaper, the air presses down with a weight of about 5 tons!

Here is how you can test the immense pressure that air exerts on large surfaces. Get a slat of wood, about the length and thickness of a yardstick. Place it on a table so that 3 inches extend over the table edge. Cover the rest of the slat with two sheets of a large-size newspaper. Smooth down the newspaper, stroking from the center of the paper out to the edges.

Now hit the end of the slat very hard with a hammer. You might expect the paper to flip up into the air. But what happens?

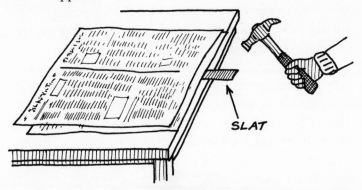

SLAT

The slat breaks. The five tons of air pressure on the paper keep it in place, and the blow breaks the wood.

Your skin has an area of more than 2,000 square inches. Since air presses with a weight of 15 pounds per square inch in all directions, the air pressure on your body is over 30,000 pounds. That is about the weight of ten full-size automobiles. How can we walk around under 30,000 pounds of air pressure?

The fact is that while 30,000 pounds of air pressure

are pushing in on your body, the same amount of pressure inside your body is pushing out. Your body is in balance. The pressure from outside is equal to the pressure from within.

What would happen if this balance were broken? To find out, you need a one-gallon metal can with a screw-on cap. Service stations often have empty oil or antifreeze cans.

The pressure on the can, you now know, is in balance. There is as much pressure from the outside as there is from the inside. To upset the balance, pour a half glass of water into the open can. Heat the water in the can until you see steam coming out of the opening. Turn off the heat and, using a pot holder, screw the cap on as tightly as possible.

Watch what happens as the air inside the can cools. The air pressure in the can goes down. The pressure outside the can is now greater than the pressure inside the can. The greater pressure on the outside crushes and bends in the sides of the can.

Air not only presses *down* with a pressure of 15 pounds on every square inch; there is pressure in all directions. In other words, air not only presses on top of your head and shoulders, but also on your face, neck, chest, back, arms, legs, hands, and feet.

Here is an amazing experiment to prove that air presses in all directions. Fill a glass to the very top with water. Cover the top with a piece of cardboard or a 3- by 5-inch index card.

What do you think will happen if you turn the glass over? Try it and see.

Carefully turn the glass upside down over a sink, holding the cover in place with your hand. Gently and slowly take your hand away. Notice how the cover stays in place. The water does not spill out of the glass. The upward pressure of air on the cardboard is greater than the downward weight of the water inside the glass.

Turn the glass so that the top faces to one side. The cardboard still stays in place, held there by the sideward pressure of the air. The side pressure is also greater than the push of the water against the cardboard.

Air is real and takes up space, even though we cannot see it. It presses on everything in all directions, even though we cannot feel it.

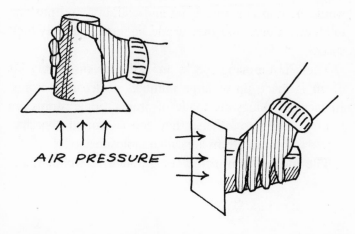

AIR PRESSURE

3
A Close-up Look at Air

What Is Air?

Suppose you had a microscope that was many times more powerful than any microscope of today, and you could look at some air through this all-powerful microscope. What do you think you would see?

You would see millions of tiny' specks. The specks would be jumping and flying and colliding and pushing in all directions. And they would be moving at very high speeds.

These fast-moving specks are called atoms. Every bit of air is made up of large numbers of separate atoms. In fact, all things are made of atoms. Some atoms are tightly joined to others; they move around together. These combined atoms are called molecules.

The molecules in some things, such as wood, stone,

metal, paper, hardly move at all. They shake back and forth, but stay in one place. These objects are solids.

The molecules in some other things, such as water, milk, gasoline, move about more. They shake back and forth more than the molecules in solids, and jump from place to place. These substances are liquids.

But the molecules in air, steam, oxygen, and so on, move even more. They shake back and forth and spring around in all directions. These are gases.

This experiment can show you that the molecules in air are always in motion. Be sure to try this experiment with the help of an adult.

Close all the doors, windows, and vents of one room of your home. The bathroom or kitchen is a particularly safe place for this experiment. Turn off air conditioners, fans, or anything else that might cause a draft in the room.

Then roll up a paper towel. Light one end with a match. Let it burn for a few seconds, and then blow out the flame.

You can see the smoke rise from the paper. It spreads out all over the room. In a few minutes, the smoke is gone.

The moving molecules in the air spread out the smoke. They bump into the tiny particles of smoke, and push them in all directions. Finally the smoke is scattered so much that it cannot be seen at all.

Blue Sky

You cannot see the air when you look across a room or across a street. The air has no color. Yet, when you look up at the sky on a clear day, you see a blue sky. Why?

We get most of our light from the sun. Light is a form of energy that vibrates, or shakes back and forth, very quickly. The speed of vibration, or frequency, determines the color of the light. Rays of blue light vibrate very fast. The other colors vibrate more slowly. Red vibrates much more slowly than blue.

Sunlight contains light rays of all colors. As these light rays, or waves, approach the earth, they bump into the molecules and particles of dust in the air. The light waves are then sent back out by the molecules and particles. The higher frequency of the blue light waves causes many more of them to bump into the air than do yellow or red light waves. The blue light goes back out in all directions.

That is why the sky looks blue on a clear day, no matter which way you face. The yellow and red rays, which have fewer collisions, come almost straight down to the earth. Therefore, the sun itself looks yellow-red in color.

Hot Air, Cold Air

You can feel the difference between hot air and cold air. But what would the difference be if you were to use your imaginary microscope to examine samples of hot and cold air?

In the cold air, you would see the vibrating molecules darting about. In the hot air, though, you would see the molecules vibrating even faster, and moving around even more. In fact, the hotter the air, the greater the speed and movement of the molecules. It is the very great activity of the molecules in the air that makes hot air feel hot.

This activity also makes hot air take up more room than cold air. As air is heated, it expands.

You can do a simple experiment to prove that hot air expands. Place a balloon over the neck of a soda bottle that is full of air only. Notice how the air stays in the bottle. The balloon hangs down.

Now stand the bottle in a pan of very hot water. The hot water heats the air in the bottle. The heated air begins to expand. Where can the hot air go? It cannot push out the sides of the bottle. It can only rise and blow up the balloon.

Remove the bottle from the heated water. As the air cools, it takes up less space. It contracts. As the air contracts back into the bottle, the balloon gets smaller, and hangs down again. ˙

You recall that air has weight. But the same amount, or volume, of air does not always weigh the same. Hot air weighs less than the same volume of cold air. Likewise, hot air fills a larger volume than the same weight of cold air.

The next experiment illustrates the two basic principles of hot and cold air: heated air expands, while cooled air contracts; and hot air weighs less than the same volume of cold air.

Take two identical balloons. Blow them both up to the same size. Tie the necks tightly so that air does not leak out. Leave one balloon at room temperature. Place the other in the freezer of your refrigerator for a few hours.

Compare the two balloons. Do you see that the one from the freezer is smaller than the one at room temperature? As the air in the freezer balloon became colder, it contracted, and the balloon became smaller.

Open the neck of the larger balloon and let out just enough warm air to make them both the same size.

Since both balloons were the same weight at first, letting air out of the warm balloon makes the warm balloon lighter than the cold balloon.

Here is another experiment to illustrate the same principle. Take two identical large supermarket bags. Open them to full size. Tape the bottom of a bag to each end of a yardstick so that the opening faces down. Tie a string to the middle of the yardstick. Hang the apparatus so that the bags are balanced and the yard-stick is level.

Now, with the help of an adult, hold a candle inside one of the bags. (Be careful not to let the flame get too near the paper.) As the candle warms the air inside the bag, it expands. The balance tips up on that side; the air inside the bag weighs less.

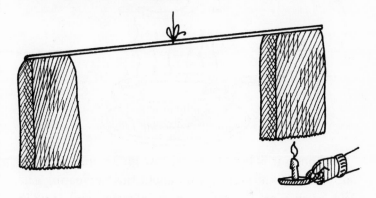

Warm air weighs less than cold air. When the two are mixed together, the warm air goes up and the cold air stays down. You can spot rising warm air in any room in your home with this special detector that you can make.

Take a piece of heavy paper about 5 inches square. Starting from the center, draw a spiral, like a snail shell, so that it fills the whole paper. The curves should be about a half inch apart. Cut out the spiral. Make a tiny hole in the center. Pass a thread through the hole, and tie a knot underneath so you can carry the spiral by the thread.

Walk around the room. Hold your spiral over a hot

radiator, a turned-on lamp, a lit stove, or even a bowl of hot food. In each case, rising warm air should make the spiral spin.

Although it is hard to see air, weigh air, and measure air, we really know quite a bit about this fascinating gas. We know that it is made up of vibrating and moving molecules. We know that the molecules in air make the sky look blue. We also know that molecules in hot air vibrate and move faster than molecules in cold air; and that hot air takes up more space than cold air, weighs less, and rises above it.

4
The Chemistry of Air

FOR THOUSANDS of years it was believed that air was an element—a single, simple substance that could not be broken down into other substances. But about 200 years ago scientists discovered that air is not an element. They found two gases in air.

They called one gas "foul air," because humans and animals could not breathe it. The other they called "fire air," because it was necessary for burning. Humans and animals could breathe the "fire air." Today we call the "foul air" nitrogen; we call the "fire air" oxygen. Nitrogen and oxygen are the two most important gases found in the air.

Nitrogen

About 78 percent of the air (78.110 percent of dry air, to be more exact) is made up of the gas nitrogen. Nitrogen has no color, taste, or odor. It is a little lighter than pure air. It does not combine easily with other chemicals to form compounds, nor does it dissolve very well in water.

Although most of the air that we breathe is nitrogen, the gas does not remain in the body. It is breathed in and right out again. If nitrogen were the only gas in the air, our bodies could not use the air we breathed and we would soon die.

Your body does not get any nitrogen from the air. But nitrogen is necessary for life. It is part of the tissue of all living things, and is found in all protein foods. You get the nitrogen you need from the plants that you eat for food. Plants get nitrogen compounds from the soil.

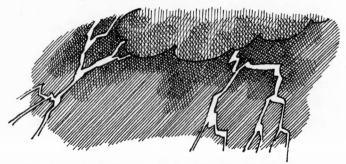

How does nitrogen get into the soil? Strangely enough, some nitrogen compounds in the soil result from lightning. The lightning forms compounds of nitrogen and oxygen in the air. Rain then washes these compounds into the ground. Other compounds of nitrogen get into the soil as dead plants, animals, and animal wastes decay in the ground. And some are produced by germs in the soil that take nitrogen from the air and change it into a form that can be taken in by the plants.

The natural amount of nitrogen in the soil is not enough for modern farming. Farmers therefore add fertilizers containing nitrogen compounds to the soil. The nitrogen used for these compounds is removed from the air by either a heat or an electrical process.

Four fifths of all nitrogen that is removed from the air is used in fertilizers. The rest is used in the manufacture of many products, from explosives to nylon stockings, and from photographic film to laughing gas— the anesthetic used by dentists.

Oxygen

Oxygen makes up the remaining part of the air—about 20 percent. (A more exact figure is 20.953 percent of dry air.) Oxygen is similar to nitrogen in that it has no color, taste, or odor. In almost every other way, it is very different from nitrogen.

Nearly every living plant and animal needs the oxygen found in the air. Every time you take a breath of air, your body removes some of the oxygen it contains. The oxygen combines with other chemicals in your body's cells to produce the energy that you need to live.

Most fuels, such as coal, oil, and wood, need oxygen in order to burn. As they burn, the oxygen in the air combines with the chemicals in the fuel to produce heat.

There is a simple way to show that oxygen is removed from the air during burning. The same experiment shows that oxygen makes up about 20 percent of the air.

Attach a small birthday candle to a bit of wood or cork. Float the wood with the candle on about one inch of water in a bowl. Light the candle, and set a large drinking glass upside down over it. Notice the level of the water inside the glass.

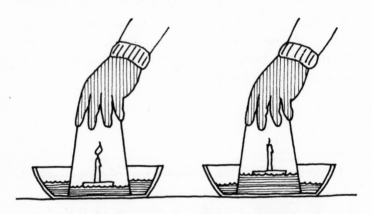

As the candle burns, it removes the oxygen from the air. The level of the water in the glass rises to take the place of the oxygen that has been removed from the air. As soon as the oxygen in the glass is used up, the candle will go out.

Notice the new level of water. The new mark is about 20 percent higher than the first mark.

Burning is not the only process that takes oxygen from the air. Oxygen combines easily with most chemical elements. Oxygen from the air combines with iron, for example, to form rust. Rusting is a joining together of iron and oxygen, usually with some moisture present, to form the compound iron oxide. To protect iron from rusting, grease or paint is applied so that air cannot reach the metal.

Try this experiment to see how rust forms.

Push a piece of plain steel wool, without any soap, into an empty small jar. Add a teaspoon of vinegar and a teaspoon of water. The vinegar removes a coating on the steel wool that prevents rust; the water helps the rust to form. Shake the liquid a few times, and then pour it out.

Now place the jar with the steel wool upside down in a bowl that has about one inch of water. Mark the level of the water that is inside the jar. Leave the setup for 24 hours.

Then check the level of the water. Did it rise about 20 percent? As the oxygen combined with the iron to form rust, the air took up less space in the jar, and the water level went up. The air inside the jar now is mostly nitrogen.

You probably know some of the more familiar uses of oxygen. Hospital patients are given oxygen to help them breathe more easily, and pilots and astronauts bring along their own supply of oxygen when they go high above the surface of the earth, where there is not enough air for them to breathe.

But did you know that one of the greatest uses of oxygen is in industry? Oxygen is used in the manufacture of iron and steel. Oxygen is also used to make the extremely hot flames needed to weld pieces of metal together or to cut them apart.

When oxygen gas is made cold enough it becomes a liquid, called LOX. LOX is used in spaceships to supply the oxygen for burning the fuel in rockets. There is not nearly enough oxygen in outer space to support the burning, so oxygen has to be carried along. It was found that the best way to carry the oxygen is as LOX.

Other Gases in the Air

Until the 1890s everyone accepted the idea that air was made up of nitrogen and oxygen. Then Sir William Ramsay and some other English scientists found evidence that there is more to air than just nitrogen and oxygen.

Ramsay actually found six more gases in air. All six are colorless and odorless and do not dissolve in water. They are also chemically inert, which means that they do not combine with any other chemical.

Ramsay found the first gas in 1894. He named it argon, from the Greek word for "lazy" or "idle." He chose this name because argon is an inert gas. Nearly one percent of dry air by volume is argon. (A more exact figure is 0.934 percent.) The greatest use of argon is in electric light bulbs. Argon keeps the bulbs burning brighter and longer.

One year later Ramsay discovered helium. It is the same gas that earlier scientists had found in the sun. The name comes from the Greek word *helios*, which means "sun." Just tiny amounts of helium are found in the air—about 0.000524 percent by volume.

Helium is very light and does not burn. It is used to inflate balloons. Also, helium mixed with oxygen makes artificial air for divers and others who must carry a supply of air with them. Most of the helium we use is made from natural gas.

Ramsay also found krypton in air. The name is based on the Greek word for "hidden." There is only a tiny trace of krypton in the air. It makes up 0.000114 percent of the total volume.

Krypton is used in photographic flashbulbs. It is also used for very exact measurements of length. An electric current is passed through krypton gas, causing it to glow with an orange-red light. The wave length of this light is the standard of length measurement throughout the world.

Neon, from the Greek word for "new," was found in 1898. Very little neon is found in the air (only 0.001818 percent of dry air).

Neon is perhaps the best known of the inert gases. It

is used in advertising signs made of glass tubes that glow with a brilliant red color. To make a neon sign, the glass tubing is bent to spell out words or numbers, or to outline a person or object. The air is removed from the tubing, a small amount of neon is introduced, and the tubing is sealed. When an electric current is sent through the tubing, the neon gas glows red.

Then came Ramsay's discovery of still another inert gas in air, which he called xenon, meaning "strange." Xenon is the rarest of the inert gases. There is only 0.0000087 percent xenon in the air—less than one ten-millionth of the total. Xenon has limited use. Mostly it is mixed with krypton for photographic flashbulbs.

It was some years before Ramsay found the final inert gas, which he called radon. Radon is a gas that is given off by radium. It is radioactive—it sends out invisible atomic particles and rays. Radon makes up so little of the air that it is called a trace element.

In addition to the six inert gases, three other gases are known to be part of the air. They are methane, hydrogen, and nitrous oxide.

Methane gas forms when plant or animal material decays without air. It is sometimes called marsh gas or firedamp. Methane is about 0.0002 percent of the air. It has no color, does not dissolve, and has almost no smell.

Hydrogen, the lightest of all elements, makes up just a tiny fraction of the air, 0.000524 percent. Although it is just a small part of air, hydrogen is the most abundant element in the universe. Scientists estimate that over 90 percent of the matter in all stars is composed of hydrogen atoms.

Nitrous oxide, a compound of nitrogen and oxygen, is also found in extremely small amounts in the air. The percentage of nitrous oxide is 0.00005. Nitrous oxide is also known as laughing gas.

Air: Compound or Mixture?

After all of the gases in air were discovered, one big question remained: How are these gases put together? Is air a compound, with all the gases chemically united? Or is air a mixture, in which the gases are just mingled together?

After many years of investigation, scientists found that air is a mixture. The gases that make up the air are thoroughly mixed together. But they are not joined by chemical bonds.

As they did their research, the scientists collected samples of air from all over the world. They tested samples from cities and from forests, from the tops of mountains and from above the ocean, and from many countries. Laboratory tests showed that the amounts of most of the gases from sample to sample were the same. Yet two gases found in the air, water vapor and carbon dioxide, did vary from place to place and from time to time.

Water vapor, a gas made up of invisible molecules of water, comes into the air as water evaporates, mainly from oceans and lakes. The amount of water vapor in the air at any time depends, in part, on the temperature of the air. The warmer the air, the more water vapor it can hold; the colder the air, the less it can hold. There can be as little as zero percent of water vapor in the air, or as much as 4 percent.

You can capture some water vapor from the air in this way. Fill a clean, dry glass with ice cubes, and let it stand for an hour or so in a room. You will see liquid water on the outside of the glass. It is drawn from water vapor in the air. It forms on the glass as the ice cubes cool the air around the glass. Since cool air cannot hold as much water vapor as warm air, the invisible molecules of water vapor combine to form drops of liquid water.

Carbon dioxide is a chemical compound made up of carbon and oxygen. Burning fuels, the breathing of living things, and decaying plants and animals add carbon dioxide to the air. Carbon dioxide, usually about 0.03 percent of the air, varies from 0.01 to 0.10 percent.

Carbon dioxide has no color or odor. It dissolves easily in water. It is about one and a half times as heavy as air. And it does not support fire. In fact, it is a perfect fire fighter. As the heavy carbon dioxide is poured on a fire, it prevents the air's oxygen from reaching and feeding the flame, and the fire goes out.

You can make some carbon dioxide at home and use it to put out a small flame.

Mix a tablespoon of baking soda and four tablespoons of vinegar in a glass. The gas you see bubbling off is carbon dioxide. Since carbon dioxide is much heavier than air, it does not escape from the glass.

Pour the carbon dioxide gas, but not the liquid, toward the flame of a candle. Observe how quickly the carbon dioxide puts out the fire.

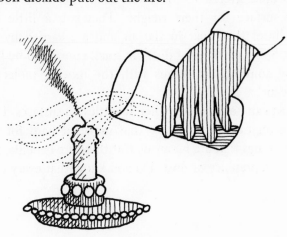

Dust

Air is made up of all the gases we have mentioned. It also contains many tiny bits of matter.

Among the particles of matter in air are sand, soot, volcanic ash, crystals of salt, seeds, molds, bacteria, bits of fabric, plastic, metal, and paper, and many others. They come from the soil, plants, fires, friction, sea spray, evaporation, and other sources. Broadly speaking, these particles are called dust.

You can see dust that has fallen out of the air. You see it on any surface that has not been used or cleaned for a period of time. The dust appears as a fine gray powder over the surfaces of things.

You can see dust in the air if you go into a dark room and turn on a flashlight with a narrow beam. The dust appears as tiny floating specks.

If dust is made of particles, why does it float in the air? Why doesn't it all settle on surfaces or the ground?

Dust particles float because they are amazingly small and light. A line of about 50,000 average-size dust particles would stretch for only one inch! Yet they have a large surface for their weight. They are a little like parachutes that float in the air and are carried by the wind. Some particles of dust are small enough to be kept up by continual collisions with the moving molecules in the air!

Dust can be annoying when it settles on surfaces. Dust in the air can cause a haze that makes it hard for you to see things that are far away. But there are benefits, too, from the presence of dust. Do you know that every drop of rain is formed by water vapor around a particle of dust? And do you recall that the sky appears blue because dust and molecules in the air scatter the light rays from the sun?

Man no longer believes that air is a single substance. Now we know that it is made up of many different substances. The two main gases are nitrogen and oxygen. There are much smaller amounts of argon, helium, krypton, neon, xenon, and radon, as well as methane, hydrogen, and nitrous oxide. Water vapor and carbon dioxide are found in varying amounts in the air. And finally there are particles of dust. All of these, together, make up the life-giving mixture that we call air.

5
Air and Living Things

Breathing In and Breathing Out

Take a deep breath. Hold it. Watch the second hand of a clock. How long can you hold your breath?

Probably not more than a minute. Scientists say that no one can go more than about 10 minutes without taking a breath.

Your body needs air to breathe. Without oxygen its cells stop working. Breathing out gets rid of the waste product, carbon dioxide, that is produced by living cells.

We breathe in and breathe out from the moment we are born until the moment we die. We do not have to think about breathing. A group of cells in our brains control our breathing. Breathing always goes on automatically and regularly.

Hold your hands on your ribs as you take a deep breath. Do you feel your ribs move up and out? The muscles in your chest expand and make the chest cavity larger. At the same time the diaphragm—the large, flat sheet of muscle that separates your chest from your abdomen—moves down. This makes the chest even larger.

When the chest expands, the lungs expand. The air in your lungs spreads out, and the pressure decreases. The pressure of the outside air is now greater than the pressure inside your lungs. The greater pressure forces air into your lungs, through your nose and mouth.

Some people have the mistaken idea that you suck in air when you breathe in. Instead, you take in air because air moves from places of greater pressure to places of lesser pressure. Air is drawn into your nose and mouth because of the lowered pressure in your lungs.

Hold your hands on your ribs as you breathe in deeply again. This time pay special attention to your ribs and chest wall as you breathe out. Do you feel your ribs move in and down as you breathe out? At the same time your diaphragm moves up, making the space in the chest still smaller. Working together, the diaphragm and chest muscles force the air out of the lungs.

Air in the Human Body

As air enters the body through the nose, it passes by tiny hairs inside the nose. The hairs act as filters—they

catch some of the bits of dust in the air. Scientists estimate that in a year each person filters out about a pound
of dust with the hairs in his nose.

The air then goes through the passages of the nose.
They are moist and warm. The passages add moisture and
warmth to the air entering the lungs.

From the nose or mouth, the air passes through the
windpipe, or trachea. The trachea enters the chest and
branches into two tubes, known as the bronchial tubes.
One tube leads to the right lung; the other tube leads to
the left lung.

Each tube divides into smaller and smaller tubes. The
air flows from the bronchial tubes to the very ends of the
tiniest tubes. Here there are small, cup-shaped struc-
tures called air sacs, or alveoli. There are hundreds of millions of alveoli in the lungs. The alveoli make up the soft
mass of the lungs.

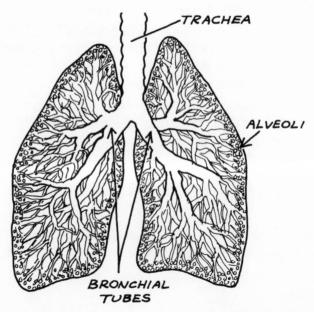

The walls of the alveoli are covered with very thin blood vessels, called capillaries. The oxygen passes through the thin walls of the capillaries into the red blood cells in the bloodstream.

The heart pumps the blood to all parts of the body. This blood is rich in oxygen. The oxygen passes from the blood through the walls of other capillaries to the cells that make up your body's flesh and bones.

The oxygen helps to burn the food in the cells at a very slow rate. The body burns the food to produce the heat and energy that it needs to carry on its growth and life cycles.

In the burning process, carbon dioxide, a waste product, is formed. The carbon dioxide is carried away by the bloodstream. The process is the opposite of the one that brings oxygen to the cells.

The carbon dioxide passes from the cells of the body through the capillary walls into the blood. It is carried by the blood to the lungs, where the carbon dioxide passes into the alveoli. Finally it goes through the branches and bronchial tubes. As the chest wall and diaphragm squeeze the lungs, the carbon dioxide is exhaled into the air.

As you sit and read this book, you are breathing in oxygen and breathing out carbon dioxide. With each breath, you take in about one pint of air rich in oxygen. With each breath you let out, you exhale about one pint of air rich in carbon dioxide.

Now put down the book. Run in place for two minutes.

Notice how much faster and deeper you are breathing.

You may be taking in as much as 4 quarts of air with every breath; that is eight times as much air as when you are at rest. And you are letting out the same amount of carbon dioxide with every breath.

When you are hard at work or play, you need a lot of energy. Your body cells need more oxygen to change the food they contain into energy. They also produce more carbon dioxide that must be removed.

Rapid, deeper breathing brings more oxygen into the body and rids the body of the carbon dioxide waste. The heart beats faster. It pumps more oxygen-rich blood to the cells. It pumps more carbon dioxide-rich blood away from the cells.

You also breathe deeper and faster, and your heart beats faster, when you are at a high altitude. The higher you go, the thinner the air—the less oxygen it contains.

The city of Denver, Colorado, is one mile above sea level. There is 15 percent less oxygen in the air than at sea level. People who live there are used to it, and breathe easily. But people who travel there from lower altitudes breathe more rapidly than usual. They need to meet the demand of their bodies for a sufficient supply of oxygen.

Air and Animals

Almost every animal on earth needs air to live. Animals all breathe in one way or another. Most animals with backbones that live on land, such as human beings, have lungs. Most fish, and other beings with backbones who live in the sea, breathe through gills. The gills are thin sheets of movable tissue, usually located behind the head.

But how do fish get oxygen, when they live largely under the water?

The fact is that water contains dissolved oxygen, and fish get their oxygen from the water.

You can easily prove that water contains dissolved air, and therefore oxygen. Fill a drinking glass with cold water and let it stand in a warm place for several hours. Cold water can contain more dissolved air than warm water. As the water warms, the dissolved air leaves the water. It appears as the many tiny bubbles you see clinging to the inside of the glass. These are bubbles of air that came out of the water.

Fish breathe by taking in gulps of water and forcing it out between their gills. As the water flows past the thin walls of the gills, the oxygen crosses over from the water to the blood that flows through the gills. From the gills, the blood carries the oxygen to the cells. In each cell, the oxygen combines with various foods, in a process similar to burning, to produce heat and energy.

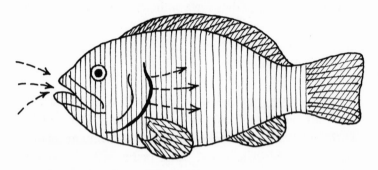

Most insects breathe through openings in their bodies, called spiracles. The air goes directly to air sacs in the insect's body. It then passes to the tissues that need it to carry on the life functions.

Some microscopic beings, such as amoebae, have no actual organs or equipment for breathing. Enough air passes through their outer skin for their oxygen needs. Man, too, obtains a tiny bit of oxygen this same way. Just under one percent of a human being's oxygen needs enters the body through the skin.

Almost all living things need air in order to live. There are, however, a certain number of bacteria, yeasts, and molds that live without air. They are called anaerobic organisms.

Anaerobic organisms are found in water, in food, in mud and soil, and sometimes in the tissue of other living beings. These organisms cause fermentation. When yeast grows in grape juice and changes it to wine, the yeast does not use any air or oxygen. Bacteria that cause tetanus, or lockjaw, grow best in an airtight puncture wound. Anaerobic bacteria are just about as common as those that require air.

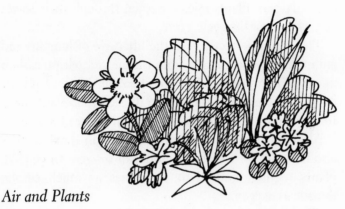

Air and Plants

Air is as necessary for plants as it is for animals. Animals require oxygen from the air. Plants, though they too require a little oxygen, need much more carbon dioxide from the air.

Plants use carbon dioxide in one of the most basic processes of life, photosynthesis. Photosynthesis means "putting together with light." In photosynthesis, food is created, or manufactured, in green plants. The plants take carbon dioxide from the air and water from the soil. They use the light energy from the sun to combine them and produce food. The food is actually a basic kind of sugar, called glucose.

All of our food comes from plants, directly or indirectly. Either we eat the plant itself, as a grain, vegetable, or fruit, or we eat animals that have eaten plants. Photosynthesis, using the carbon dioxide from the air, is the basis of nature's entire food chain.

In photosynthesis, plants take in carbon dioxide and water to produce glucose. But photosynthesis also produces oxygen. Plants release oxygen through their leaves as part of their life cycle.

This fits in perfectly with the life cycle of humans and animals. We take oxygen from the air and release carbon dioxide. The plants take in carbon dioxide and release oxygen. We produce the carbon dioxide that plants need to live; plants produce the oxygen that we need to live.

Although plants mostly require carbon dioxide, they also have use for a certain amount of oxygen. In general, plants require more than ten times as much carbon dioxide as oxygen.

The oxygen that plants take in from the air is used to burn the glucose that is formed in photosynthesis. This provides the plant with part of the energy it needs to live and grow.

You can prove that plants need air in this experiment. Spread a thin layer of Vaseline over the tops and bottoms

of four leaves of a house plant. The coating of Vaseline prevents air from reaching the leaves. Within a day or two, you will notice that the coated leaves have lost their color and are beginning to wither.

Wipe the Vaseline off two of the leaves. If you do it soon enough, the leaves will start to breathe again. They will get back their green color and normal appearance. The leaves that are still covered will soon die altogether nd fall off.

Air is a vital factor for all forms of life. It allows life to go on. It is also important in photosynthesis, the basic production of food on earth.

6

The Atmosphere

THE PLANET earth is surrounded by a blanket of air. This cover of air is called the atmosphere. As the earth moves through space, the atmosphere moves with it. Just as you are held on the earth's surface by the force of gravity, so the atmosphere is also attracted to the earth by gravity.

The air of the atmosphere goes up about 600 miles. Above that there are vast spaces between the molecules that make up the air. Each molecule is like a Ping-Pong ball bouncing around in an empty gymnasium.

Scientists think, though, that the earth's gravity extends to air molecules up to a height of about 18,000 miles. Higher than that, molecules are free of the earth's gravity, and do not move with the earth. So we say that the atmosphere is about 18,000 miles deep.

You know that the air is most important in sustaining

life. But do you know that the atmosphere is also a re-markable shield and protection for living things?

The atmosphere protects us from the approximately 100 billion meteors from outer space that strike the earth every day. Most meteors are the size of a grain of sand. A few are the size of large boulders.

If a large meteor were to strike a city, it would cause great destruction. But most meteors are burned up as they pass through the atmosphere. They are burned up by the friction caused by rubbing against the air particles. They finally come down to the earth's surface as harmless dust.

The atmosphere also protects the earth from the dangerous invisible rays and beams that head toward the earth from outer space. These rays could cause widespread disease and death among living things. It is possible that life as we know it could not exist without the protection of the atmosphere against these rays and beams.

The atmosphere further serves to keep the earth at a comfortable temperature. During the day, the atmosphere protects us from the full power of the sun's rays; during the night, it conserves heat that has been received from the sun by trapping it near the surface. Without the atmosphere, our blood would boil by day and freeze at night.

The Layers of the Atmosphere

The atmosphere is usually thought of as four separate

layers of air. The bottom layer, closest to the solid surface of the earth, is called the troposphere. Above it are the stratosphere, the ionosphere, and the exosphere. Beyond the exosphere is outer space.

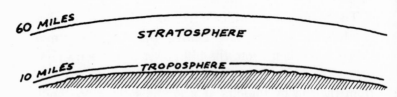

The word "troposphere" is Greek in origin. It comes from a word that means "turning" or "changing," and refers to the moving winds and changing weather conditions within this lowest layer of the atmosphere.

The troposphere extends above the earth 5 to 10 miles at various places. Above the colder spots on the earth, near the north and south poles, the troposphere reaches up only about 5 miles. Above the warmest spots on the earth, along the equator, the troposphere goes up to about 10 miles.

About 80 percent by weight of the total amount of air in the atmosphere is in the troposphere. All the weather —winds, rain, snow, and storms—is found here. The air of the troposphere contains great amounts of water vapor and dust, too.

The air is thickest and heaviest at sea level, the lowest level of the troposphere. As you go higher and higher, the air becomes thinner and lighter. Pilots use the drop in air pressure as they fly their planes up, to measure their height, or altitude. The lower the pressure, the greater the altitude. The altimeter is an instrument that measures the air pressure and shows the result as feet of altitude.

The greater the height in the troposphere, the colder the air. The temperature of the air drops about three or four degrees Fahrenheit for every thousand feet of altitude. In some spots over the United States, the temperature at the top of the troposphere goes down to about −55 degrees F. Over the equator, the temperature of the air at the top of the same layer drops to −100 degrees F. because of the greater height there of the troposphere.

There is a limit beyond which the temperature does not drop any further. When you cross this imaginary border, called the tropopause, you leave the troposphere and enter another layer of air. This second layer is the stratosphere. The word comes from the Latin and means "layer" or "covering." The stratosphere extends some

50 miles above the troposphere. The air here is much thinner than in the troposphere; there is much more space between the molecules.

The stratosphere is a quiet level—there is no weather there. It is in the stratosphere, though, that ultraviolet rays from the sun strike molecules of oxygen in the air. Many of the rays are stopped in this way.

The molecules struck by the ultraviolet rays contain two atoms of oxygen. The ultraviolet rays split the oxygen molecules into separate oxygen atoms. Then, when a single oxygen atom collides with an oxygen molecule containing two oxygen atoms, it forms a three-atom molecule. Oxygen molecules with three atoms are called ozone.

Ultraviolet rays can be dangerous to man. They can give you a sunburn if you are out in the hot sun too long.

Too much exposure to ultraviolet rays may even lead to skin cancer. It is lucky that most of the ultraviolet rays from the sun are stopped by the ozone in the stratosphere.

The bottom of the stratosphere, about 10 miles above sea level, is very cold: it is about −67 degrees F. At 25 miles above sea level, however, it can be as hot as 100 degrees F. above zero. The heat is caused by the collisions between the ultraviolet rays and the oxygen molecules. Above this level, though, the temperature drops again. At the top level of the stratosphere, called the strato-pause, the temperature is down to about −20 degrees F.

Still higher is one of the most fascinating layers of the atmosphere, the ionosphere. The name comes from the large number of ions, or electrically charged atoms and molecules, found in this layer. The word "ion" comes from a Greek word which means "to go" or "to wander." The ionosphere extends from about 60 miles up to 300 miles above sea level.

The air is very thin in the ionosphere. There are vast spaces between the molecules and atoms.

The molecules and atoms in the ionosphere are con-stantly being struck by atomic particles and rays from outer space. In addition to the light rays from the sun, there are also powerful radio waves from the sun as well as from other stars and sources in outer space. There are also streams of atomic particles from the sun and from other stars and meteors. And there are cosmic rays from beyond our solar system.

The molecules and atoms in the ionosphere start out in electrical balance—they are neutral. But as these molecules and atoms are struck by the atomic particles and rays from outer space, all sorts of atomic accidents take place. Molecules are split apart, electrons are knocked off atoms, and so on. The molecules and atoms now are torn apart and are out of balance: they have either a plus or a minus electrical charge. They have become ions.

The ions in the lower part of the ionosphere have a remarkable property. They are able to reflect radio waves beamed out from the earth. Without this blanket of ions, a radio broadcast would be heard only by people who lived within sight of the radio station. Since the ionosphere reflects the radio waves, they bounce back and forth between the ionosphere and the surface of the earth. They can be heard all around the world.

The reflecting part of the ionosphere is quite complicated. It has several different layers; each one reflects either shorter or longer radio waves. Also, the reflecting property of each layer changes depending on the position of the sun. In general, the layers reflect more during the day than at night.

You can see how the ionospheric layers change with this experiment. Sometime during the day, tune your radio to an AM station. Tune it carefully to receive the station as clearly as you can. Turn off the radio, and ask that no one use it for the rest of the day.

Then turn it on again late at night. You will probably have some trouble receiving the station. When the sun set, the level of the ionosphere changed. Now you must retune the radio to get the station as clearly as before.

Try to get radio programs from distant cities. It is often easier at night to pick up broadcasts from stations that are hundreds of miles away.

AM radio waves are very long waves, so they are reflected by the ionosphere. Television waves, though, are much shorter. They pass right through the ionosphere and go out into space. Therefore television waves that are being sent a great distance either must go through a wire or cable, must be sent along a row of towers no more than about 40 miles apart, or must be sent up to a satellite in space which beams the waves back to the earth.

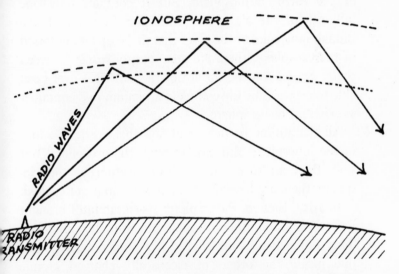

During the fall or spring, if you live in a far northern area, you may see a glowing or flickering green or red light in the sky. This is called the aurora borealis. (If you live far south in the Southern Hemisphere, the similar light there is called the aurora australis.) These lights are in the ionosphere, about 70 miles above the extreme north and south of the earth. They are believed to be caused by atomic particles hurtling into the upper atmosphere at speeds of thousands of miles a second.

As you approach the top of the ionosphere, some 300 miles above the earth's surface, the temperature rises to about 2,000 degrees F. It is at this level that the highest and largest layer of the atmosphere begins—the exosphere. It reaches from the top of the ionosphere up to about 18,000 miles above the earth's surface.

The exosphere contains 99 percent of the total volume of the earth's atmosphere. But it contains only one billionth of the air in the atmosphere by weight. Although molecules of the gases that make up air are found in the exosphere, there are great empty spaces between them. No one on the surface of the earth has ever been able to create as nearly complete a vacuum in a container as exists in the exosphere.

All the atomic particles and rays that create the ions in the ionosphere also pass through the exosphere. But since there are so few molecules and atoms in the exosphere, there are few collisions, and few ions are created.

In 1958, though, the Explorer space satellites brought back some astounding information about the exosphere. They found two bands, shaped like immense doughnuts one inside the other, of electrically charged atomic particles. The inner belt extends from about 1,000 to 3,000 miles above the earth. The outer belt goes from about 8,000 to 12,000 miles. Since much of the research concerning these belts was done by Dr. James A. Van Allen, they are called the Van Allen belts.

Not much is known about the Van Allen belts. It is believed that they are held in place by the earth's magnetic field. It is also believed that the atomic particles in the belts come from the sun, from cosmic rays, and

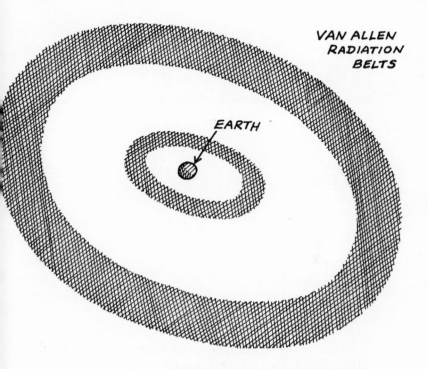

EARTH

from test explosions of atom and hydrogen bombs in the upper atmosphere. One of the objects of future space exploration is to learn more about the Van Allen belts.

The top of the exosphere is defined as the highest point at which air moves with the earth: about 18,000 miles higher than sea level. Above that, the few isolated air molecules and atoms move about freely—they do not move with the earth. It is the beginning of outer space, the vast emptiness through which the stars and galaxies travel.

7
Wind

WIND IS the movement of air from one place to another. Winds are created in several ways.

Air can be pushed to make a wind. When you blow out a candle, when you wave a fan, or when you turn on an electric fan, you are pushing the air and creating a wind.

You can also make a wind by changing the temperature of the air. If you heat air, it becomes lighter; the warm air rises up over the cold air. This movement is wind. And if you chill air, it becomes heavier and pushes in under the warmer air, also making a wind.

You see many winds that are created by changes in the air temperature. Most of them show warm air rising over colder air.

Look at a smoking chimney. The smoke goes up because it is mixed in with the air that has just been heated

in a furnace or fireplace. Look at the air above the kitchen stove when water is boiling. You can see the steam going up as the air over the stove is heated and rises. Watch what happens when a match is lighted. Notice how the smoke rises as the flame heats the air. Can you think of other winds that are created by changes in temperature?

Finally, when an area of high-pressure air moves into an area of low-pressure air, there is wind to make the pressure equal all over. As the air moves, a wind is created.

You can hear a wind caused by change in pressure when you open a can or jar that has been vacuum sealed. In vacuum sealing, most of the air is removed from the can or jar, creating a very low air pressure inside. As you break the seal, the high-pressure air outside rushes into the area of low pressure.

You can create this kind of wind the next time you take a hot bath or shower. Keep the door to the bathroom closed as you bathe. The hot water warms up the air in the room. The warmer air has less pressure than the cooler air in the other rooms.

Now quickly open the bathroom door. You will feel a wind. It is caused by air rushing from the higher-pressure area outside into the lower-pressure area inside the bathroom.

Sometimes the air is moving but you cannot feel it. You can try this experiment to prove that the air in your house is moving, or circulating, even though there is no wind.

You need the help of an adult to do this experiment. It works best during cold weather. Close all the windows and doors in a room. Then open one window about 2 inches at the top and 2 inches at the bottom. Roll a paper towel into a tight tube. Standing near the window, light one end with a match. Let it burn for a few seconds, and then blow out the flame.

Hold the smoking towel near the open top of the window. What do you see? Now hold the towel near the open bottom of the window. What do you see here?

The smoke escapes through the top part of the window because warm air rises. At the bottom of the window the smoke is blown into the room. In part this may be caused by the wind. But even more important is the fact that the air outside is colder than the air inside; it has a higher pressure. It is pulled into the room through the opening at the bottom of the window.

Winds on the Earth

The temperature of the air is affected by the heat of the sun. Along the equator, the sun's heat makes the air very hot. Near the poles, the air gets less heat from the sun.

As the air along the equator is warmed by the sun, it expands. It becomes light and rises.

When this warm air gets up into the upper atmosphere, it is cooled and becomes heavier. It begins to drop to a lower level.

The air cannot drop straight down, though, because other air is being warmed and lifted over the equator. Instead, it goes down on a curved or sloped course. It heads toward either the north or the south.

As the warmed air over the equator rises, it creates a belt of low pressure. The colder, high-pressure air north and south of the equator pushes in to make the pressure equal.

This completes the cycle: Air at the equator is warmed and rises. When it reaches the upper atmosphere it is cooled, and slides down toward the north or south. This air is then pulled toward the low-pressure area at the equator—and the cycle starts all over again.

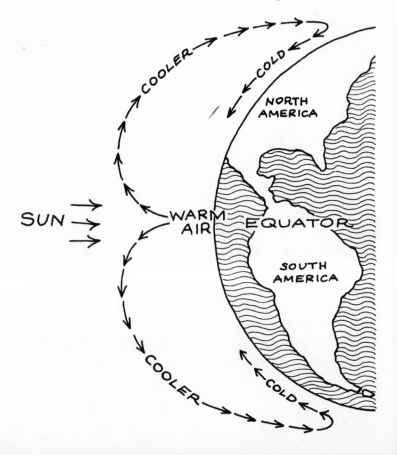

If you could see this air movement from outer space, it would look like a giant fountain in slow motion. The air goes straight up along the equator. It curves out, and falls back at some distance from the equator. Then it flows in toward the equator, where it is sent up again.

This air movement sounds quite simple. Really it is much more complicated, because all of this is happening around the planet earth—and the earth itself is spinning around in space. The spinning of the earth has very important effects on the winds—the movement of the air. Here is one such effect.

Suppose that you were able to squeeze the earth, making it as flat as a phonograph record. The poles would then be in the center of the disk; the equator at

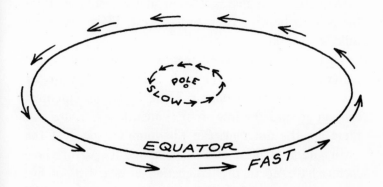

the outside edge. If you put a record on a phonograph and turn it on, it spins. Points on the outside (the equator) move very fast. Points closer to the center (the poles) move more slowly.

It is the same with the spinning earth. A spot on the equator spins very fast. The closer a spot is to one of the poles, the more slowly it spins.

The air over the equator spins very fast, too. As this fast-moving air rises over the equator and heads toward the north or south pole, it passes over parts of the earth that are spinning more and more slowly. The air now is moving faster than the land beneath it.

Since the earth spins from west to east, this air is moving faster in that direction than the land is. People on the surface feel the moving air as winds blowing from west to east. They are called west winds, since winds are named after the direction from which they come.

The air coming back down from the poles is spinning more slowly than the places it passes on its way toward the equator. This makes it seem that the cold air from the poles is blowing from east to west. These winds are called east winds.

There are, then, several factors that shape the wind patterns on the earth. There is the rising of warm air and sliding down of cool air. There is the movement of cool air toward the low-pressure area of warm air. And there are the differences in the spinning speed of the earth and the speed of the air above it. All of these factors have led to the designation by scientists of five belts, or zones, of wind patterns.

Wind Belts

There is little surface wind at the equator. The air

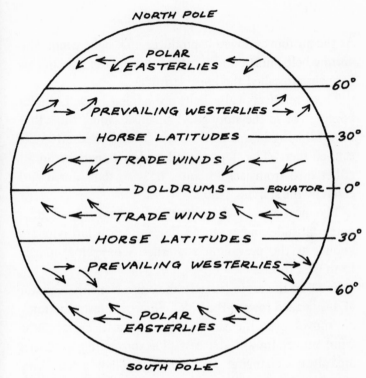

slowly rises as it becomes heated. This area is called the doldrums, meaning "dull space," because of the lack of winds.

The trade winds are found just north and south of the equator. They fill two belts stretching from the doldrums to about 30 degrees north and south latitude. The trade winds are steady and moderate. The name comes from an old German word that means "steady" or "on course."

The trade winds blow toward the equator; they are moving in to replace the rising warm air. They blow in an easterly direction on both sides of the equator.

At about 30 degrees north and south latitude, some of the air that rose over the equator returns to the surface.

As the air moves down, it produces only light wind. The narrow belts, north and south of the equator, where this happens are called the horse latitudes.

These relatively calm belts are named horse latitudes because (or so the story goes) Spanish sailing ships that were bringing horses to the New World were often becalmed there. The ships moved so slowly that the horses either died from lack of water or were slaughtered and eaten by the starving sailors.

The next wind belts, from about 30 to 60 degrees north latitude and 30 to 60 degrees south latitude, are known as the prevailing westerlies. They blow mostly from west to east.

Some of the air in these belts comes from the equator and is headed toward the poles. Since this faster-spinning air moves over the slower-spinning earth surface, the wind moves toward the east. The prevailing westerlies are always changing and shifting. They often bring storms and bad weather.

The last two wind belts extend from 60 degrees north latitude to the north pole, and from 60 degrees south latitude to the south pole. They are known as the polar easterlies. They start the trip of the cold air toward the equator. Again, the slower-spinning air over the faster-spinning earth tends to make them blow from east to west.

Local Winds

The five wind zones cover the general circulation of air all around the earth. But the oceans and continents,

the mountains and valleys, the seasons, day and night—
even big cities and factories—also affect air movement.
They create the local winds.

The land mass of Asia, for instance, is warmed more
than the surrounding seas by the sun in the summer. The
warm air over the land rises. Cool air from the sea rushes
in to fill the low-pressure area. This causes a wind,
known as the summer monsoon—from the Arabic word
for "season."

In the winter, the land cools off quickly; the oceans
lose their heat much more slowly. The air over the ocean
now is warmer, and rises. Air rushes from the land to the
sea, from high to low pressure. This causes the wind
known as the winter monsoon.

Every summer day, the same sort of thing takes place
on the shores of oceans and large lakes all over the
world. During the day, the hot sun warms the land more
than the water; the wind blows cool air from over the
water to the land. At night, the water keeps its heat
longer; the cool air from over the land blows toward the
water. That is why it is cooler and more comfortable near
the water on hot summer days and nights.

Wind Speed

The winds on the earth blow at rates from calm to as high as 500 miles per hour. In 1806 a British admiral, Sir Francis Beaufort, devised a scale to estimate wind speed by observing objects in the wind. Here is the Beaufort Scale:

NO.	MILES PER HOUR	DESCRIPTION	OBSERVATION
0	0–1	Calm	Smoke goes straight up.
1	1–3	Light air	Smoke drifts; no change in weather vane.
2	4–7	Light breeze	Wind felt on face; leaves rustle; weather vane shifts.
3	8–12	Gentle breeze	Leaves and twigs move; light flag extends.
4	13–18	Moderate breeze	Dust, scrap paper rise; small branches move.
5	19–24	Fresh breeze	Small trees sway.
6	25–31	Strong breeze	Large branches move; telephone wires whistle.
7	32–38	Moderate gale	Large trees in motion.
8	39–46	Fresh gale	Twigs break off.
9	47–54	Strong gale	Some damage to buildings.
10	55–63	Whole gale	Trees uprooted; structural damage.
11	64–75	Storm	Widespread damage—felt at edges of hurricanes and tornadoes.
12	over 75	Hurricane or tornado	Massive destruction.

Look out the window. Guess the speed of the wind.
Now turn on the radio and listen to the weather report.
Compare your guess with the official speed of the wind.
How close were you?

Wind speeds of more than 75 miles per hour mean
that there is a major storm in the area. If the wind is
blowing at from 75 to 200 miles per hour, the storm is
known as a hurricane. When these storms form in the
Pacific Ocean, they are called typhoons.

Hurricanes form over the oceans during very hot
weather. They have a typical spiral shape that may extend for hundreds of miles. The powerful winds, the
drenching rains, the high tides and blown water of a
hurricane usually cause a great deal of damage.

The fastest winds of all are in tornadoes. No one has
been able to measure a tornado wind. It is believed to
be between 300 and 500 miles per hour.

The path of a tornado is small. On the average, it is
about ¼ mile wide and 16 miles long. The tornado
moves forward at about 40 miles an hour. It passes in a
minute. But it can easily destroy anything and everything in its path. On April 11, 1965, thirty-seven small
tornadoes struck in the Midwest: approximately 250
people lost their lives, 5,000 were injured, and property
damage came to $300 million. On April 3, 1974, nearly
100 tornadoes struck a wide area from Georgia to
Michigan. Almost 350 people were killed, with many
thousands more injured. Property damage was over $1
billion.

Tornadoes are also called twisters. They have an easy-
to-recognize funnel shape. The destruction is caused by

the high winds that whip around the outside of the funnel, and by the partial vacuum in the center of the funnel.

Winds can be cool and refreshing, or harsh and damaging. They can carry the weather great distances. They create waves in the ocean; they blow away the topsoil from improperly used farmland. For good or evil, wind is an important feature of the earth's atmosphere.

8
Weather

You can tell whether the weather is hot or cold, windy or calm, rainy or snowy, cloudy or clear. But do you know what makes the weather the way it is?

The weather is determined by the air around us. If the air is cold and dry, the weather is clear and sunny; if the air is warm and humid, the weather is cloudy and perhaps showery; and so on.

All of the movements and changes in the air that make up the weather take place in the lowest few miles of air, in the troposphere. The air here moves about in great masses that can cover thousands of square miles. There can be as many as fifty air masses covering the earth at any moment.

Some air masses stay in one place—they hardly move at all. Others move at speeds of thousands of miles a day. Some masses quickly change or disappear as they move about and bump into other air masses; others do not change for many days and over many thousands of miles.

There are four basic types of air masses. The cold, dry air masses form over cold land areas, such as northern Canada. After getting chilled for a few days, and with almost no moisture at all, the cold, dry air mass heads south. It brings clear, dry weather with it. There are few clouds, light winds, and excellent visibility.

The warm, humid air masses form over a warm body of water, such as the Gulf of Mexico. The air is warmed and picks up a great deal of moisture. A warm, humid air mass carries with it great numbers of clouds and rain showers.

If an air mass forms over a cold ocean, it is cold and humid. When this air mass passes over mountains it often drops its moisture, as rain in the summer and as snow in the winter. Cold, humid air masses are very welcome in the summer—they usually bring relief after a hot spell.

The fourth kind of air mass contains warm, dry air. It usually comes from a tropical land area. The warm, dry air mass is recognized by clear skies with no rain or snow, and extreme differences of temperature between day and night. The temperature changes lead to strong, gusty winds.

When a cold air mass moves over an area, it usually slides in under the warm air that is there already. It forces the lighter warm air up and away. The forward surface of the cold air mass is called a cold front. A cold front often means stormy weather, with rain, strong winds, and perhaps thunder and lightning.

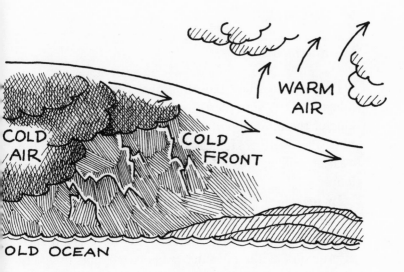

COLD
AIR

COLD
FRONT

WARM
AIR

OLD OCEAN

A warm front is the forward surface of a warm air mass. When it enters an area, it usually slides over the cold air, since warm air is lighter than cold air. As it continues to move in, it pushes out the cold air. There are likely to be clouds and either rain or snow along a warm front. But it is usually a steady fall or showers, rather than the violent storms that go with a cold front.

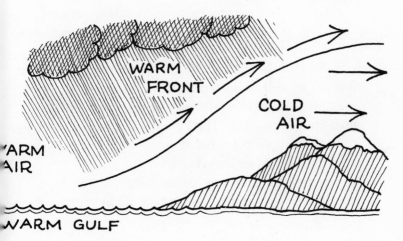

WARM
FRONT

COLD
AIR

'ARM
AIR

WARM GULF

Weathermen

People who study the atmosphere are called meteorologists. They are experts in the science of the weather. One of the most important jobs of the meteorologists is to make weather forecasts. Forecasts tell what the weather will be like over the next day or two, or even longer.

In making a forecast, the meteorologist tries to determine which air masses and fronts will be shaping the weather in his area. He bases his forecast on such information as the pressure, temperature, and humidity of the air, both at the surface and at various heights in the atmosphere; the direction and speed of the wind at different altitudes; the percentage of the sky covered by clouds; the amount of any rain or snow that falls; and so on.

But it is not enough for the meteorologist to know the weather in his area alone. He must also find out what the weather is like hundreds and thousands of miles from his station. He wants to know how weather patterns are changing, how the air masses are moving, and which ones are heading toward his station.

At each of about 300 stations of the National Weather Service, as well as on the high seas and in other countries, the meteorologists use various instruments to measure the weather. This information is then sent in code form to all the other stations. Each meteorologist bases his forecast on these facts.

Meteorologists inform airline pilots of the kind of weather they can expect along their flight routes. They

advise farmers on when the first frost will arrive. They warn parkway police of an approaching storm. They also give the weather reports over radio and television, so that people will know what clothes to wear, or if it is a good day to go to the beach.

Meteorologists measure the temperature with a thermometer. The simplest thermometer has a thin column of alcohol or mercury in a glass tube. As the temperature rises, the liquid expands and goes higher up in the tube. Numbers marked beside the tube show the degrees of temperature.

THERMOMETER

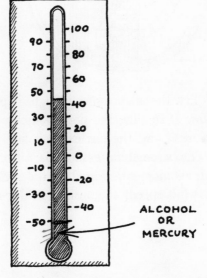

ALCOHOL
OR
MERCURY

Meteorologists today actually use a more modern thermometer that measures the temperature by electricity.

The meteorologist measures the air pressure with a barometer. The type most often used is the aneroid barometer. It consists of a small, sealed box made of flexible metal. The air is removed from the box, and a stiff spring keeps it from collapsing. A metal pointer is attached to the top of the box.

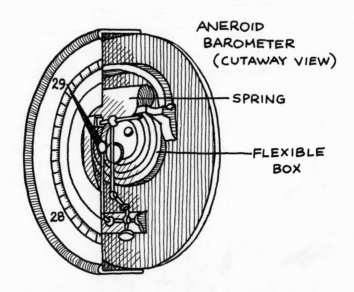

ANEROID
BAROMETER
(CUTAWAY VIEW)

— SPRING

—FLEXIBLE
BOX

When the air pressure is high, it presses on the box, making it smaller; the pointer moves down. When the pressure is low, the box expands and the pointer moves up. The barometer measures the air pressure in this way.

An anemometer is used by the meteorologist to measure wind speed. It consists of three round cups that extend out from a metal frame. The wind spins the cups around. The stronger the wind, the faster the cups of the anemometer whirl. Electrical contacts measure the speed in miles per hour.

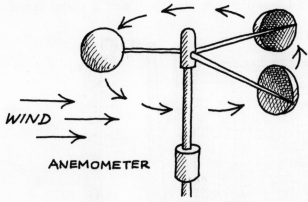

WIND

ANEMOMETER

A weather vane is usually a flat piece of metal that is shaped to a point at one end. It is attached to a pole so that it is free to turn in all directions. As the wind blows, it pushes the weather vane to point the direction from which the wind is blowing.

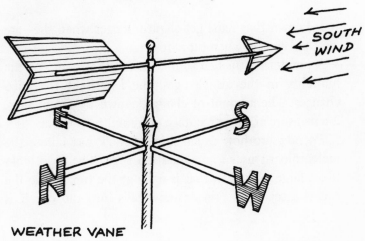

SOUTH WIND

WEATHER VANE

Humidity is a measure of how much water vapor, or moisture, is in the air. The meteorologist often uses a hair hygrometer to measure humidity.

The hygrometer has several hairs—usually blond human hairs—that are stretched over a metal frame.

HYGROMETER

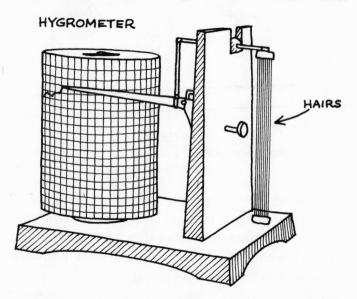

HAIRS

It is known that hairs get slightly longer when they are wet, and shorter when they are dry.

A pointer is attached to one end of the frame. As the humidity in the air changes, the length of the hairs changes. The amount of change, shown by the pointer, is a measure of the percentage of humidity in the air.

To measure how much rain or snow has fallen, the meteorologist uses a precipitation gage. The gage looks like a large metal can that is open at the top. Inside the can is a scale. As rain or snow falls into the can it is weighed. The increase in weight is a measure of how much rain or snow fell.

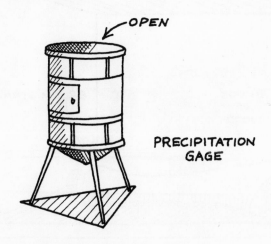

PRECIPITATION
GAGE

Your Own Weather Station

Even though today's meteorologists use advanced electrical instruments in modern weather stations, you can make your own weather observations with home-made weather instruments.

First you need to make an instrument shelter. Place a large wooden or cardboard box on some sort of stand. Be sure that it is about 4 feet above ground level and away from any building or wall. Set the box so that one side can be opened and closed; this side should face north. Poke a few small holes in each of the sides so that air can circulate through the shelter.

The thermometer is the only instrument that you need to buy or borrow. Place an outdoor thermometer in the shelter to measure the temperature.

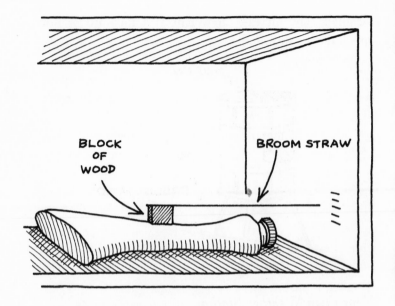

BLOCK OF WOOD

BROOM STRAW

Make your own aneroid barometer to measure changes in air pressure. Take a clean empty plastic detergent bottle. Smear glue around the mouth of the bottle. Squeeze as much air as possible out of the bottle to make a partial vacuum inside. Screw the cap on very tightly over the gluey mouth of the collapsed bottle to seal it. Changes in air pressure now will make the bottle expand and contract.

Glue a small block of wood to the middle of the side of the bottle. Glue a broom straw horizontally onto the wood. The straw is the pointer of the barometer.

Place your barometer on its side in the shelter, with the end of the straw pointing to one side of the box. Listen to a weather report on the radio, and mark down the official air pressure at the level your straw now points to. Do the same thing once a day for about a week. By the end of the week you will have several set points to use as a scale of air pressure. As the air pressure changes, you will notice that the pointer has gone up or down. You will be able to read the approximate pressure from the scale on the box.

A hair hygrometer will give you a measure of the moisture in the air. Cut a square of heavy cardboard about 12 inches wide and 12 inches long. Get a single hair that is at least 10 inches long, and set it aside. Make a pointer about 6 inches long out of oaktag or thin cardboard. Use a pencil to poke two small holes, one above the other, in the blunt end of the pointer.

Carefully tie one end of the hair through the lower hole. Then push a thumbtack through the other hole to attach the pointer loosely to the cardboard near the top. Next poke another thumbtack slightly into the cardboard about 6 inches below the hole through which

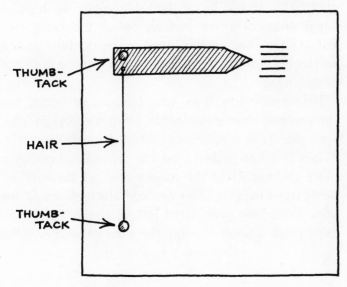

the hair is tied. Pull down on the hair until the pointer is straight from side to side. Tie the loose end of the hair to the bottom thumbtack and push it firmly into the cardboard.

Stand your cardboard hygrometer in the shelter against one wall. Find out the humidity from the radio, and mark that percentage on the cardboard where the pointer is pointing. Each day put a mark where the pointer points, so that you have a scale of humidity on the cardboard. You will find that the less the humidity, the higher the pointer; the greater the humidity, the lower the pointer.

To make your own anemometer, knock a headless nail into the center of a board the size of this book or larger. Let at least 1½ inches of the nail stick up. Place a plastic straw over the nail.

Next staple three light plastic (or plastic-covered) cups to the edge of a paper plate or an aluminum pie plate. They should be on their sides along the edge, at equal distances apart, and all facing the same way. Balance the plate on the straw, as you carefully push a nail with a head through the plate and into the open top of the straw.

Before mounting it on your instrument shelter, you can calibrate your anemometer. On a windless day, ask your parents to take you and a friend for a short drive. When it is safe to do so, ask the driver to go exactly 5 miles an hour. Hold the anemometer out the window, being very careful of other cars and obstructions. At the same time, have your friend look at a watch and time exactly one minute. Count the number of times the

anemometer turns during the minute. Repeat the pro-
cedure at 10 and 15 miles an hour, and write down your
results. You will then have a scale for measuring wind
speed by counting the number of turns of the anemometer.

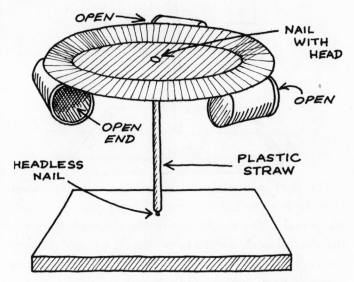

The weather vane also begins with a board and a
headless nail, hammered into the center with 1½ inches
sticking up. Mark the four directions, *North*, *West*,
South, and *East*, along the four edges of the board.

Use scissors to cut out the flat center part of an
aluminum pie plate. Cut a 2-inch-wide strip from it,
and shape one end to a point. Staple the center of the
strip to one end of a plastic straw. (Use two staples.)
Place the straw over the nail in the board.

Mount the entire weather vane on top of your instrument shelter. Be sure that the side of the base marked

North is facing in that direction. As the wind blows, your weather vane will point toward the direction from which the wind is blowing. You can then read the direction of the wind.

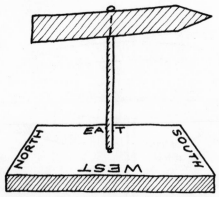

The final measuring instrument that you may want to make is a precipitation gage. Simply place an empty one-pound coffee tin on top of the instrument shelter, too. After it rains, insert a ruler into the can and measure the depth of the water. Each inch of water in the can indicates about one inch of fallen rain.

You are ready to make some observations now. The only other thing you need is a weather chart to enter the figures. A weather chart is also very easy to make.

Mark off two wide columns and six narrow columns on a sheet of white construction paper. Write *Date and Hour* at the top of the first wide column. Enter here the exact time of each observation. Head the second wide column *Clouds*. Describe here how much of the sky is covered by clouds. The following six columns should be *Temperature, Air Pressure, Humidity, Wind Speed, Wind Direction,* and *Precipitation*.

Try to make daily observations of weather conditions at the same hour each day; you will be better able to compare the weather from one time to the next. You will also be able to compare your findings with the figures

WEATHER CHART

DATE & HOUR	CLOUDS	TEMP.	AIR PRESSURE	HUMIDITY	WIND SPEED	WIND DIRECTION	PRECIP.

from the National Weather Service. Perhaps you will notice patterns in the weather. You may even be able to forecast the weather on the basis of your observations.

Following the weather reports and forecasts every day can be fun. Making your own instruments and using them to be an amateur meteorologist can be even more fun.

9
Air at Work

Sailboats

People have always watched the winds, and learned to live with them. But as far as we know, it was not until a few thousand years ago that someone had the idea of putting wind to work, by building a sailboat.

The first sailboat was probably made in ancient Egypt about 5,000 years ago. It consisted of a large square of cloth hung from a pole in the front of a boat. As the wind pushed on the cloth, the boat moved through the water.

These early boats could move only with the wind, that is, in the direction in which the wind was blowing. About 2,500 years later, boats began to be built with the mast and a movable sail in the middle of the boat. They also had a rudder—usually an oar held in the water behind the boat—to steer them in the right direction. Now it became possible to sail across the wind, and even to go against the wind.

To sail a boat across the wind, the sail is held at an angle. Part of the wind's force can then be used to push the boat in the right direction. The rudder and the keel, the flat board on the hull that extends straight down, prevent the boat from being pushed sideward. Sailboats can actually go faster across the wind than with the wind.

A sailboat cannot sail right into the wind—the sails flap about and the boat hardly moves at all. To go against the wind, the boat must be sailed in a zigzag course. This is called tacking. In tacking, the boat cuts across the wind one way and then the other, but always moves ahead at the same time in the opposite direction to the wind.

You might enjoy making your own simple sailboat from scrap materials. Use a flat piece of wood for the hull. Attach a tall, thin stick upright in the middle for

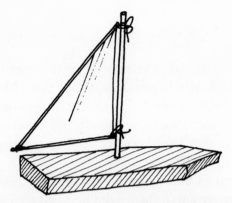

the mast. Now attach a piece of cardboard or cloth stretched over a frame of thin wooden strips to the mast.

Place your home-made sailboat in a pond or even a large puddle. Now check the speed and direction of the wind. How does the wind affect the movement of your boat? Does the wind stay the same or does it change? Sail your boat at different times. Are the wind conditions different?

Windmills

The invention of the windmill, about 1,500 years ago, was an important step forward for our civilization. In the windmill the force of the wind is used to produce mechanical power.

In the typical windmill, four sails of cloth or four blades of wood or metal are attached to a gear mechanism. The blades are set at an angle to the wind. As the wind turns the blades, the gears turn.

Small gears turn the larger gears. Rods or wheels attached to the large gears are used to run various kinds of machinery. A windmill with 10-foot blades can build up about one horsepower in a 20-mile-per-hour wind.

The first windmills were used to pump water, for

irrigating farmland. The most popular use of the windmill, though, was to grind grain into flour. Much later,
windmills were connected to electrical generators to produce electricity. Today windmills are hardly used. In
most cases they have been replaced by gasoline engines
and electric motors.

Children all over the world, though, still enjoy playing
with a toy version of the windmill, called a pinwheel. To
make a simple pinwheel, you need an 8-inch-square piece
of paper, a straight pin or tack, and a pencil with an
eraser at one end.

Match one corner of the paper to the opposite corner;
then fold the paper in half on the diagonal. Open up the
folded paper, and fold over the opposite corners. Open
up this fold, too. The paper now has two folds, and
where they cross is the center of the paper.

Cut along each fold to within ½ inch of the center.
Now you have four cuts and you have eight corners.

Bend one of the corners over so that the tip covers
the center of the paper. Hold it there with your finger.
Skip the next corner, and bend the following corner
over in the same way as the first corner. Slip this corner

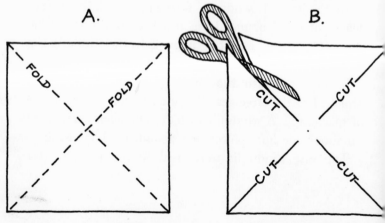

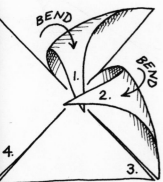

under your finger, too. Twice more, skip a corner, and bend the next one over and slip it under your finger.

You are holding four corners in place with your finger. Take the pin and push it through the four corners and also through the center of the paper. Then push the pin through the rubber eraser on the pencil. Push it in just far enough so that the pinwheel can turn.

Make the pinwheel turn by blowing on one of the wings. Do you see how the pinwheel catches the wind and is turned? Blow very lightly, and then very hard. How fast can you make the pinwheel spin?

Kites

Historians guess that the very first kites were made in ancient Greece about 2,400 years ago. A kite is made of paper or cloth stretched over a lightweight frame. It is held by a long length of string.

The string is attached so that the kite is held at an angle. The wind strikes the face of the kite, and pushes the kite up and away against the pull of the string. The

balance between the push of the air and the pull of the string holds the kite aloft.

Sometimes you want to fly a kite but there is little wind. You can increase the speed of the wind by running into the wind, holding the kite behind you. This pulls the kite against the wind; the wind presses harder on the face of the kite, making it fly up into the air.

Compressed Air

Air that is squeezed into a small space is called compressed air. Compressed air is air under pressure. It pushes hard to spread out and lessen the pressure.

You can compress air in the following way. Blow up a balloon about half full. Push the balloon into an empty small food can. Place the cut lid on top of the balloon, and press the end of a ruler down lightly on the lid. As the air in the balloon is squeezed, it spreads out to fill the entire bottom of the can. By how many inches does the ruler reach into the can?

Continue to press on the lid and compress the air inside the balloon. The harder you press, the smaller the balloon, and the stronger the push against the ruler. How much farther does the ruler go down?

What happens if you press too hard? The balloon bursts. The compressed air pushes so strongly that it breaks the thin skin of the balloon.

Try this experiment to observe the great strength of compressed air. Place a balloon on a table near the edge. Let the neck of the balloon dangle over the side. Place a book on top of the balloon.

Now blow into the balloon. Notice how the book rises up from the table. The weight of the book further compresses the air going into the balloon. The highly compressed air pushes hard enough against the book to raise it off the table.

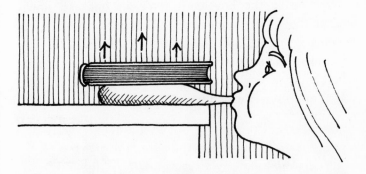

Every time you bounce a ball you are using the principle of compressed air. The rubber ball is filled with air. As it hits the ground, it gets pushed in on one side. This squeezes, or compresses, the air, which pushes against that side, and the ball bounces up.

The tires on a car are filled with compressed air. A pump squeezes a lot of air into the tires. The compressed air pushes with enough force to hold up the great weight of the car.

The noisy air hammer that is used to break up concrete is powered by compressed air. Compressed air powers the automobile lift that raises cars up so that mechanics can work below. Spray cans use compressed air. You use a pump to force compressed air into air mattresses to blow them up. Air brakes in trucks; air rifles; the caissons used to build tunnels under water—all these use compressed air.

One of the newest and most interesting uses for compressed air is in the hovercraft, or air-cushion vehicle. These vehicles actually travel on a cushion, or layer, of air.

Fans inside the hovercraft force air out and down against the surface underneath. The air is squeezed between the surface and the bottom of the vehicle. The cushion of air supports the weight of the vehicle anywhere from a few inches to 2 feet above the ground, water, or rails over which it runs.

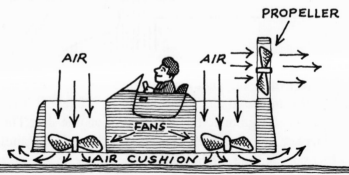

The forward motion of the hovercraft comes either from propellers, as in a plane, or by changing the direction of the airflow beneath the vehicle. There is an air-cushion train in France that is pulled along the rails by magnetism.

Vacuum

When you lower the air pressure inside a closed space, you create a vacuum. You can do this in three ways: remove the air, make the space larger, or cool the air.

These ways lower the air pressure; but they cannot create a perfect vacuum. They cannot remove absolutely all the air from a space. They can only create partial vacuums.

When there is a partial vacuum in a closed space, the pressure of the air outside is greater than the air pressure inside. The outside air rushes into the partial vacuum whenever it can. We use this property of air in several ways.

When you breathe in, you make your chest larger. The amount of air in it now fills a larger space. The pressure is lowered; you have created a partial vacuum. Air from the outside now rushes in to make the pressure inside the same as the pressure outside.

The air pump that you use to blow up a bicycle tire or a football works the same way. By pulling the handle up, you make the space inside the pump larger. This lowers the pressure and creates a partial vacuum, and air from the outside is pulled into the pump. By pushing

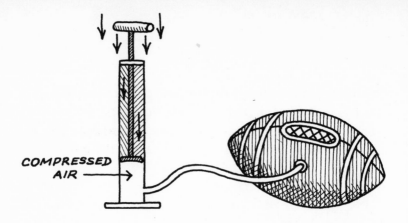

COMPRESSED AIR →

the handle down, you make the space inside the pump smaller. This compresses the air, and forces it out through a tube to fill the tire or ball.

A vacuum cleaner also works by pulling in outside air. The lower pressure is caused by a spinning fan which pushes the air in one direction. At the same time, air is pulled through a hose on the other side of the fan.

The incoming air carries dust and dirt with it. The debris is caught and held in a cloth or paper bag. The air, though, goes right through and out the other side of the vacuum cleaner.

The Thermos, or vacuum, bottle, shows another use of partial vacuum. We use a Thermos bottle to keep hot liquids hot or cold liquids cold for as long as 24 hours. It consists actually of two glass bottles, one within the

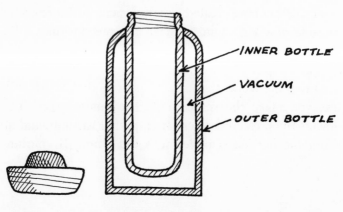

INNER BOTTLE

VACUUM

OUTER BOTTLE

other. The space between the bottles is sealed and the air is removed, creating a partial vacuum.

This vacuum cuts down very much the exchange of heat between the inner bottle and the outer one. It keeps the liquid, whether it is hot soup or ice water, at the same temperature for a long period of time.

The experiment described on page 8 shows that by allowing warm air sealed in a can to cool, you create a partial vacuum inside the can, causing it to collapse.

There is a partial vacuum in the picture tube of your television set; it reduces the number of collisions between the electrons that form the picture and molecules and atoms. There could be no television picture without the partial vacuum in the picture tube. Water pumps use a partial vacuum to draw water up from wells and into buildings. Gasoline flows in the automobile engine because of a partial vacuum. You even create a partial vacuum when you sip soda through a straw!

The Push and Pull of Moving Air

Hold your hand in front of your face. Blow on your hand. Do you feel the increased pressure? Moving air has a greater pressure in the direction in which it is moving.

Now try this experiment. Tie two apples to two 12-inch lengths of string. Attach the other ends of the strings to a rod. Let the apples hang from the rod about 2 inches apart. Blow on one of them. It swings forward, pushed by the increased pressure of air.

But what happens when you get close to the apples and blow hard into the space between them?

The two apples move toward each other.

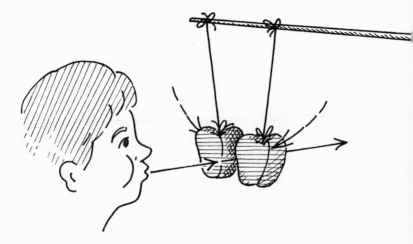

The pressure along a moving stream of air goes down as the speed of the air increases. The apples are pulled together because as you blow you create a stream of air that is moving faster than the surrounding air. Therefore the air pressure between the apples is lower than the pressure of the air surrounding them, and they come together.

A perfume atomizer works in this same way. The liquid perfume is in a small glass jar. A thin tube goes down into the jar. On the top of the jar is a rubber bulb that can be squeezed, and a nozzle through which the perfume escapes.

When you squeeze the bulb, a stream of air crosses inside the top of the bottle. This lowers the pressure in the bottle, and a tiny bit of perfume is pulled up the tube. The moving stream of air pushes this perfume forward, and it comes through the nozzle as a fine spray.

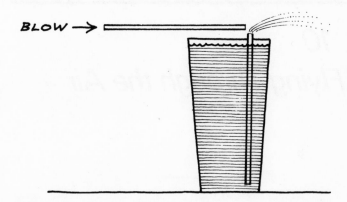

You can make your own atomizer. Fill a tall glass with water. Place a straw in the water. Cut its length so that just a tiny bit of the straw extends above the water.

Next take another straw. Hold it perpendicular to the top of the straw that you are holding in the water, and blow through it across the top of the straw in the water.

A spray of water goes out of the glass. The drop in pressure caused by the moving air pulled the water up through the vertical straw.

People have found a great many clever ways to put air to work. Air is used to push and pull, sail and fly, clean and spray, lift and bounce, keep cool and keep hot, shoot a bullet and stop a truck, bring you good clear pictures on TV, and do many more tasks.

10
Flying Through the Air

FROM EARLY times on, people have dreamed about flying. They looked at the birds, and tried to fly as they did. But they soon found that their muscles were not strong enough to allow them to flap any of the winglike devices that they might attach to their arms.

Over the years there were many different ideas for human flight. One of the most interesting was Leonardo da Vinci's invention, around 1500, of a type of helicopter. It had a screwlike blade above its body. Historians believe that Leonardo built a small model of his helicopter, and that he was able to set it in flight.

Balloons

The first person actually to fly was carried up by a balloon on October 15, 1783. The balloon was made by two brothers in France, Jacques and Joseph Montgolfier. They got the idea from watching smoke rising from a chimney.

At first they filled paper balloons with smoke from a straw fire, and watched them fly. Later they learned that it was not the smoke but the hot air from the fire that made the balloon lighter than the surrounding air, so that it would rise. In the Montgolfiers' first man-carrying balloon, damp straw was burned in a fire pan at the narrow opening to the balloon to produce the hot air.

Hot air, though, was not the ideal gas for balloons. Many paper and cloth balloons caught on fire because of the burning straw. Also, the air in the balloon would

cool, and the balloon would come down, as soon as the fire went out.

Today we have toy balloons that fly, as well as large ones that are used for weather research and other purposes. They are filled with helium, one of the gases found in the air.

Helium is quite a bit lighter than air itself, and it provides the lift balloons need. Hydrogen gas, which is even lighter than helium, had been used for a while. But hydrogen ignites and explodes very easily. Helium was found to be a much safer gas for blowing up balloons.

For some years after the first balloon flight, balloons were used for sport, for scientific studies, and for military purposes. Races were held to see who could go the highest, travel the farthest, and stay up the longest. Many experiments performed in the upper atmosphere used balloons to get scientists and scientific instruments up off the earth. As late as World War I, balloons were used to observe enemy troops and to direct cannonfire.

Airplanes

Still, people dreamed of flying like the birds. On December 17, 1903, Orville Wright flew the first successful heavier-than-air flying machine, which he built with his brother Wilbur. The basic design of the Wright brothers' airplane is still in use today. It looks very much like a bird in flight.

The Wright brothers' plane and all planes built since then are the same in two important ways. They have a lightweight engine that either pulls or pushes the plane through the air; and they have wings to give the plane lifting power.

The Wright brothers' plane used one 12-horsepower engine to turn the two propellers. The propellers pulled the plane forward at a speed of less than 7 miles an hour. Most of today's planes use four jet engines, each with over 5,000 horsepower. They push the plane forward at speeds of more than 500 miles an hour.

The plane's wings help provide lifting power. The front of the wing is slightly higher than the back. As the engines move the plane through the air, the air presses on the bottom of the wing and pushes it up.

You can try this out. Hold a piece of paper by one edge. The paper hangs down. Now move your hand quickly through the air from one side to the other. Do you see the paper rise? It rises because the air is now pressing on one side of the paper, pushing it up.

The shape of the wing also adds to its lifting power. If you look closely at an airplane wing, you will notice that it is curved out on top and flat on the bottom.

As the plane moves, the air on top of the wing must go faster to get over the curve than the straight-flowing air underneath. You recall that faster-moving air has a lower pressure. The reduced pressure above the wing therefore pulls the wing up. It lifts the entire plane.

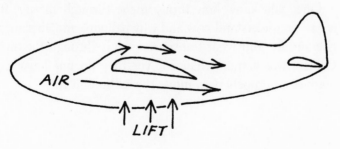

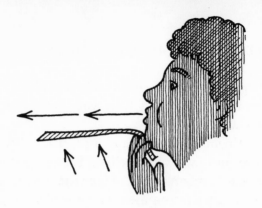

You can see for yourself how this works. Cut a strip of paper about 8 inches long and 3 inches wide. Hold one of the ends against your chin, just under your lower lip. The paper hangs down. Now blow straight out. That moves the air above the paper.

The moving air has lower pressure. Since the pressure beneath the paper does not change, the paper is pulled up to the lower-pressure area. Do you see the paper rise and extend nearly straight out in the air?

These two forces—air pressing on the bottom of the wing, and the lower pressure above the wing—keep an airplane in the air. About one third of the lifting power comes from the air pressing on the bottom, two thirds from the reduced air pressure above. That is how air can support giant planes that weigh many, many tons.

Gliders

Once you know how things move through the air, it is easy to understand how and why balloons and airplanes rise and fly. But what transports gliders through the air? Gliders weigh more than air, yet they do not have jet engines or propellers to move them through it.

Gliders use several scientific principles to help them fly. They weigh very little—they are made usually of plywood with a cloth covering. They have extremely long wings to provide maximum lifting power.

To make up for the lack of an engine, a glider must be launched before it can fly. It is either pushed off the side of a hill or first towed along the ground by a car or powered plane, or by a launching winch. Pulling the glider by car, plane, or winch is like getting a kite up into the air by running with it. The air presses on the surface of the object being pulled—kite or glider—and pushes it up into the air.

Once he is up, the glider pilot looks for rising currents of air. White, fleecy cumulus clouds are a good sign: they are usually formed by rising warm air. The pilot flies beneath the cloud, and is lifted up by the rising air currents. Air currents that rise over hills and mountains also lift a glider. Cities and freshly plowed fields are usually warmer than the surrounding areas, and therefore produce rising currents of warm air. For the opposite reason, lakes and forests, which are relatively cool, usually signal downward currents of air.

Glider pilots have set some remarkable records. Gliders have risen to nearly 9 miles above the earth. They have traveled distances as great as 650 miles. And they have flown at speeds as high as 80 miles an hour!

Our knowledge and understanding of how to fly through the air have given "wings" to man, and fulfilled the centuries-old dream.

11
Air Pollution

THE HALLOWEEN parade in the small Pennsylvania town of Donora is an important event. Firemen, policemen, and Scouts march; bands from all over the area play; and dozens of children in fancy costumes ride their decorated bicycles.

But the Halloween parade on October 29, 1948, was different from all the other parades in Donora. On October 27, a thick mixture of smoke and fog, called smog, had settled into the valley where Donora is located. This was not terribly strange. There are several large steel and zinc mills in town, and their smoke often combines with the valley's fog to create smog. But usually, wind or rain clears away the smog in a day or two.

This time, though, the smog hung on over Donora day after day. In fact, it kept getting worse. By the day of the parade, the smog was so thick that the onlookers could barely see the paraders—who were only some 15 feet away!

During the parade Donora's eight doctors worked without stop. Older people, infants, and those suffering with heart or lung disease were having great difficulty in breathing. Firemen left the parade to rush oxygen to people who were choking for air. The town's sixty hospital beds were quickly filled with patients struggling to breathe. The first deaths directly caused by the smog were reported.

It was not until two days later that relief came. A rainstorm struck, and washed the smog away. Only then could Donora total up the human damage caused by the five days of smog: of a population of 14,000, nearly 6,000 had become sick because of the smog. And some 20 people died because they had no pure air to breathe.

This was the first air pollution disaster recorded in the United States. There have been many similar disasters in other parts of the country, and around the world. The earliest one was in London, England, in 1873; it resulted in some 650 deaths. The Meuse Valley, in Belgium, in 1930 had a five-day smog condition that left 60 dead. New York City had an episode in November 1963, when officials estimated that between 200 and 400 deaths had been caused by the pollution. The worst air pollution disaster of all time was in London in 1952. During the five days of smog, there were over 4,000 extra deaths!

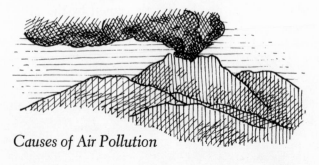

Causes of Air Pollution

Disasters from serious air pollution conditions make big headlines in the newspapers. But few people realize that the dangers of air pollution are everywhere. There are very few spots, if any, on the face of the earth where the air is completely pure. The air you are breathing right now is more polluted than the air your parents breathed when they were your age. And it is much, much more polluted than the air your grandparents breathed.

Smoke, gases, and dust in the air cause air pollution. Air pollution is harmful to your health, comfort, and safety; and it prevents you from using and enjoying the outdoors.

A small part of the world's air pollution comes from natural causes—volcanoes throwing gases and debris particles into the air, leaks of natural gas, and the smoke and gases that are produced when a bolt of lightning starts a forest fire. Most air pollution, though, is caused by man. And most of the pollution that man adds to the air comes from the things that he burns.

Right now, Americans are adding about 300 million tons of pollutants to the air every year. Of this amount, nearly half—close to 150 million tons—comes from cars and trucks. Another 50 million tons come from the burning of fuels to heat homes and other buildings, and to generate electricity.

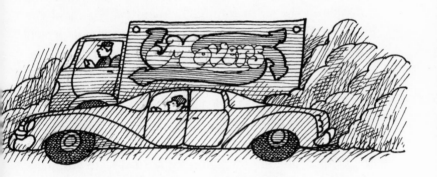

About 40 million tons of pollutants are thrown into the air from manufacturing plants as a result of their industrial production. Another 15 million tons result from the burning of solid wastes. The final 45 million tons come from various other sources, ranging from brush fires started by man to insecticide sprays.

There are, then, five major sources of air pollution: motor vehicles, heating and power plants, factories, waste disposal, and miscellaneous causes.

Types of Air Pollution

There are also five major types of pollutants. The greatest single pollutant is the gas carbon monoxide (CO). In fact, nearly 150 million tons of CO go into the air every year. About half the total pollution in America is caused by CO. CO is produced when a fuel, such as gasoline, coal, or oil, is not completely burned. If the burning conditions are right, so that there is enough heat and a good supply of air, the fuel is completely burned; then relatively harmless carbon dioxide (CO_2) is produced. If not, carbon in the fuel joins with oxygen in the air to form CO. About two thirds of the CO in the air comes from cars and trucks in which gasoline is incompletely burned in the engine.

Carbon monoxide has no odor, no taste, and no color. But it is a deadly poison to man, even in small amounts. When CO is inhaled, it takes the place of the oxygen in the blood, and so reduces the amount of oxygen carried to the cells in the body.

People suffering from lung or heart disease are made much worse when the level of CO in the air rises. There is enough CO in the air of most large cities around the world to cause headaches and dizziness. Continued exposure to CO can actually cut a person's ability to think and reason. And if the level gets too high, it can lead to death.

Compounds of sulfur and oxygen, called sulfur oxides, make up about 45 million tons of the yearly pollutants. These gases are produced when fuels containing sulfur are burned. Electric power plants and industrial plants are the largest producers of sulfur oxides. They burn immense amounts of coal and oil, which contain sulfur as an impurity. The air pollution disasters in Donora and elsewhere were largely the result of high levels of sulfur oxides in the air.

Sulfur oxide pollution can be reduced in two ways. One way is to burn only high-quality fuels containing less than one percent sulfur. The other is to remove the sulfur oxides from the gases produced by burning.

Sulfur dioxide (SO_2) is the most important of the sulfur oxides. In large amounts it has a sharp, irritating smell. When we inhale air containing SO_2, it irritates the entire breathing system, from the nose to the lungs. Some of the SO_2 in the air combines with other gases to form powerful sulfuric acid (H_2SO_4). Sulfuric acid can do great damage to the delicate tissue of the lungs.

The sulfur oxides are bad not only for human health; they also destroy plants. Many plants, in fact, are more sensitive to the sulfur oxides in the air than are humans. Sulfur oxides injure plant tissue and lead to small-sized plants and low crop yields.

Property is also damaged by the sulfur oxides. Much of this damage is caused by the highly destructive sulfuric acid. It eats away, or corrodes, such metals as iron, steel, and zinc. It discolors and damages building materials, such as brick, stone, glass, and marble. And it destroys many other items, such as clothing, paper, and leather.

The hydrocarbons are a group of pollutants produced by fuels that are not burned completely. About 45 million tons are added to the air every year. Over half of the total comes from car and truck engines that do not work perfectly.

Hydrocarbons are not themselves poisonous in the amounts usually found in the air. But they add to air pollution in another way. The light energy from the sun combines the hydrocarbons with other pollutants in the air to form a new and different group of pollutants, called photochemical oxidants.

The photochemical oxidants produce the smelly, brown haze of polluted air. They also irritate the eyes, nose, and throat and make breathing difficult. In addition, photochemical oxidants block the sunlight and damage plants.

Tiny particles of matter also cause air pollution. Americans alone add 40 million tons of such particles to the air every year. These include tiny bits of ash, soot, metal, soil, germs, and plant material, as well as liquid and solid chemicals. They range in size from those visible only under a powerful microscope, to those you can see with the naked eye.

Most of these particles come from burning fuel and from the processes of industry. For instance, steel mills produce about one ton of dust for every ten tons of steel that they turn out.

Some particles are very tiny and light. They float about in the air for long stretches of time. Every time we take a breath, we take in some of these particles. But sooner or later most particles come down. Then they make us feel dirty; they soil our clothes and put a coating of dust and grime on trees, plants, buildings, and everything else, outdoors and in.

Scientists have recently begun to find some of the possible health hazards of air that is polluted with particles. They have examined the lungs of people who lived in areas of high particle pollution, and found them covered with bits of dirt. The particles also seem to carry the poisonous gases into the lungs. Scientists have noticed that when the pollution level of particles and sulfur oxides goes up, the number of people who get sick with breathing difficulties and the number of deaths among the elderly go up too. Also, there is suspicion of a link between a high level of particles of matter in the air and some forms of cancer.

The last major group of air pollutants is the nitrogen oxides—mainly nitrogen dioxide (NO_2). Nearly 25 million tons of nitrogen oxides are added to the air every year.

The nitrogen oxides are produced when fuel is burned at a very high temperature and then allowed to cool quickly. Nitrogen in the air does not usually combine with other chemicals. But under great heat nitrogen and oxygen combine to form various nitrogen oxides. If these gases are cooled slowly, the elements separate; but in quick cooling, the nitrogen and oxygen remain together as a nitrogen oxide.

Not much is known about the long-range health effects of the nitrogen oxides. One study linked the level of nitrogen oxides in the air with the number of cases of flu among children. In the presence of sunlight, the nitrogen oxides combine with hydrocarbons to form the highly irritating photochemical oxidants.

There has been air pollution since the first volcano erupted. But over the centuries man has multiplied the causes of pollution many times over. His automobiles, airplanes, factories, furnaces, and power plants are today's major sources of pollution.

Weather and Air Pollution

For a long time, man did not suffer from all the pollution he created. The atmosphere was able to take in all the pollutants and spread them about so that they did no harm. Even now, the wind blows away most pollutants and the rain washes them out of the air, so that pollution seldom reaches a dangerous level.

But from time to time the weather does not help to get rid of pollution. Then there can be a pollution disaster, similar to the one that struck Donora.

Most of the time the air near the surface is warmer than the air higher up. The warm air rises and the cooler air drops down, to be warmed and rise in turn.

There are winds as the air moves about. Sometimes, though, a mass of warm air forms above an area. The cooler surface air is trapped in place; it does not rise. This situation is called a temperature inversion. Some cities, such as Los Angeles, have frequent temperature inversions; others have them just from time to time.

During a temperature inversion there are only weak breezes. But life goes on as usual, and more and more pollutants are added to the air—with nothing to carry them away. This leads to the high levels of air pollution that sicken or kill people, animals, and plants, and damage or destroy property.

Air pollution has become one of mankind's major problems. It threatens our health and general well-being. It has become a matter of international concern. People all over the world are now joining in the challenging fight against air pollution.

12
Fighting Air Pollution

MANY PEOPLE are involved in the fight against air pollution. Legislators are writing and passing new laws. Scientists are studying pollution and developing ways to control it. And the public is showing its concern about the need to breathe clean, pure air.

In 1970, the Environmental Protection Agency (EPA) was set up. This federal agency works against all kinds of pollution. It works to end air pollution. It also works against water pollution, noise pollution, solid waste pollution, and so on. Part of the EPA's work is to help the state and local antipollution agencies in their efforts.

The EPA controls air pollution according to standards set up in the 1963 Clean Air Act. This law sets the allowable limits of pollution from many sources. The prime targets, though, are automobiles and electric power plants. These two sources are among the largest contributors to air pollution in our country. A drop in the pollution they produce will significantly reduce the total amount of air pollution.

EPA inspectors see to it that everyone, including car makers, power plant operators, factory owners, and the public, complies with the standards. Most people cooperate willingly. If they do not, the inspectors can call on the courts to force individuals and companies to obey the law.

Working with the inspectors are air pollution scientists and their helpers. They test air samples that are collected by the inspectors, to determine what pollutants the samples contain. They use automatic testing stations to keep a continuous watch on the air quality of an area.

Air pollution scientists also do basic research into the causes, results, and prevention of pollution. They search for better automobile engines, furnaces, and industrial plants that can operate without adding to pollution. They test the effects of air pollution on people, animals, and plants. They look for ways to protect living beings and objects against damage by pollutants in the air. They do research on the different levels of pollution, and suggest standards for safe levels.

Scientists, their helpers, and inspectors make up most of the workers in pollution control. But there are many others who also do important work. There are writers who prepare books, booklets, and newspaper and magazine articles on pollution. Their job is to inform the public about the dangers of pollution. They tell people how they can fight pollution.

There are lawyers who use the courts and the legal

system to stop the violators of pollution laws. There are educators who teach and lecture in schools and before clubs and other organizations. They bring facts and explanations to those who are interested in learning more about pollution. And there are park rangers, conservationists, and others who are involved in pollution control as part of their daily work.

Air Pollution Emergency

Many city and town governments have plans for dealing with an air pollution emergency. Usually these plans include steps to prevent the emergency from developing. There are also procedures to follow in case there is an actual emergency.

The local pollution agency keeps a close watch on the pollution levels in the air from day to day, or even hour to hour. The agency also keeps track of weather conditions and forecasts—the weather can determine the course of an air pollution emergency.

The agency knows the chief sources of pollution in an area. It has information about the kinds and amounts of pollution that they create. In case of an emergency, it knows which types of pollution need to be reduced immediately. It keeps doctors and hospitals, police and fire services, as well as the public informed on the situation as it develops.

At the heart of most emergency plans is a four-stage schedule of action. Stage one is the forecast stage. It is called for when the weather forecast shows the possibility of a temperature inversion or other weather situation that might cause a pollution emergency.

The second stage is the air pollution alert. An alert is called if any one of the pollutants is present in the air in a dangerous amount, or if the weather is not likely to clear the air within 12 hours.

During the alert stage, the burning of garbage and other open fires are banned for most of the day. Power plants and factories are warned to cut back their operations. The public is told to drive less, and to use less electricity so the power plants can burn less fuel.

If the danger continues, the area enters the third stage: the air pollution warning. The ban on fires continues. Industrial sources of pollution must cut back even more. The public is told how to avoid the ill effects of air pollution.

In an air pollution warning stage, it is best to stay indoors if possible. The air indoors is usually much cleaner than outdoors. It is also wise to avoid exertion. The more active you are, the harder you breathe; the harder you breathe, the more pollutants you take in. People are also encouraged not to drive, to turn down the heat in their homes, to use less electricity, and not to use the phone so that emergency messages can get through.

The final stage is the air pollution emergency. Pollution is so high at this stage that there is a danger to public health. All nonessential pollution sources must stop working. Cars and trucks are not allowed on the road except for emergency trips. Public, commercial, and industrial buildings close down. The public is told how to act during the emergency.

Fortunately, pollution levels have seldom reached this fourth stage in recent years. The four-stage plan has helped communities to control the dangers of pollution and to avoid serious health hazards. Perhaps provision for such a plan in the past might have prevented the tragic air pollution disaster in Donora.

13
What You Can Do About Air Pollution

THE Environmental Protection Agency and the state and local pollution control agencies are doing all they can to reduce the amount of pollution in the air. But they need the help of all people who want to breathe clean air.

One of the ways you can help is by learning more about pollution. You have read about the causes of pollution, and the steps that are being taken to fight it. Here are some activities that will show you how you can measure the amount of pollution in the air.

Measuring Smoke Density

Here is how you can measure the darkness, or density, of smoke. Watch a chimney or smokestack that is releasing smoke into the air. Decide how dark you think the smoke is, on a scale that goes from 1 to 4. Write down "1" if the smoke is pale gray, "2" if it is darker, "3" for very dark, or "4" if the smoke is completely black.

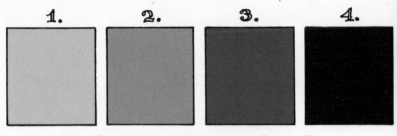

SMOKE DENSITY SCALE

Observe the smoke once a minute for 5 minutes. Each time decide if it is pale, dark, very dark, or black. Write down the proper number. Also write the number of times you saw smoke of that shade.

Enter the numbers on a chart like the one below. Then multiply the two figures for each shade of smoke. Add up the answers. Divide by 5—the number of observations. Multiply the result by 20, to get the percentage of smoke density.

SHADE OF SMOKE		NO. OF TIMES SEEN		ANSWER
1	×	2		2
2	×	1		2
3	×	2		6
4	×	0		0
			TOTAL	10

$10 \div 5 = 2$

$2 \times 20 = 40\%$ smoke density

This chart was made at a town dump where solid wastes were being burned. The percentage of smoke density from the dump was 40. This indicates a very high, unhealthy level of smoke in the air.

The air pollution inspectors employed by government agencies judge density in much the same way. But there are too few inspectors to do the job. They welcome reports from citizens concerning buildings that are emitting very dense smoke into the air. These buildings are violating the law. Alert citizens can bring the violators to the attention of government inspectors.

If you are interested in helping professional air pollution inspectors, write to your local air pollution agency. Ask for a copy of the Ringelmann Chart. It will help you measure the darkness of the smoke even more accurately. If you report your findings to the air pollution agency, be sure to include the date, time, and speed and direction of the wind for each observation you make.

Counting Particles in the Air

This experiment can give you an idea of the number of particles of matter present in the air that you breathe. You need ten 3- by 5-inch index cards and a wide roll of white masking tape.

Number the cards from 1 to 10. Cut ten 4-inch strips from the tape. Now take each strip, fold the two ends back, and attach them to an index card so that the sticky side faces out.

With other tape, attach the cards to the outside and inside of five windows. (Try to use windows facing in

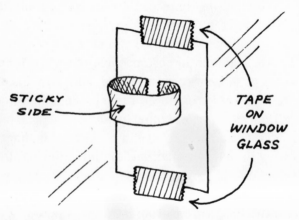

STICKY SIDE

TAPE ON WINDOW GLASS

different directions.) Make a chart with the following columns: *Card Number, Location* (inside or out), *Direction Window Faces,* and *Results.*

Leave the cards in place for a day or two. Then collect them. Examine the pieces of tape for the particles of pollution they have captured.

Compare the cards. What differences do you see between the inside and outside cards? Between cards that face in different directions? Can you explain the differences? Was the outside card with the most particles facing a source of pollution, such as a road with heavy traffic, a factory, or a power plant?

Mark off a ¼-inch square near the center of each piece of tape. Using a magnifying glass, count all the particles you can see in the marked-off square. (You should be able to see particles that are one thousandth of an inch or larger.) If there are 15 or fewer particles, the air is clean; if more than 100 particles, the air is badly polluted.

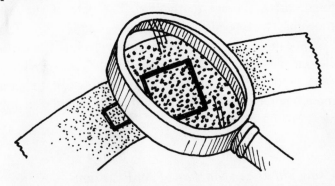

The exhaust from an automobile contains both gases and particles that pollute the air. The gases are carbon monoxide, hydrocarbons, and nitrogen oxides. Most of the particles are of the metal lead. Lead is added to gasoline to make cars run more smoothly.

To prove that auto exhaust contains particles, attach a strip of tape to another index card. Hold the card about one foot from the tailpipe of a car that has its motor on but is parked. Do this experiment out of doors, not in a garage. Don't breathe in the fumes, and make sure the driver knows you are there.

Write up your experiment. Include the make and year of the car, the date of the last tune-up, the type of gasoline used (regular, high-test, or lead-free), and the number of particles on the card.

Repeat the experiment with other cars' exhaust. Try the experiment before and after a car has been tuned up. See if there are differences between cars that use regular gasoline and those that use lead-free gasoline.

When you have done ten tests, arrange your findings in a chart. What conclusions can you come to? How important is the age of the car? The date of the last tune-up? The type of gasoline used?

You can do the same experiments collecting the particles on glass slides that are covered with Vaseline. Then you can look at the slides through a microscope, to get a more complete count of the number of particles in the air.

Using Plants as a Measure of Air Pollution

Plants that have been exposed to pollution in the air show signs of leaf damage. The worse the pollution, the more damage to the leaves, and to the plant. If the pollution level is very high, the plant dies.

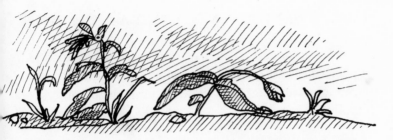

Some plants are better indicators of pollution than others. Scientists have found that the tobacco plant and the white-flowered petunia are especially sensitive to photochemical oxidants in the air. Other plants that show clearly the damage caused by photochemical oxidants are bluegrass, tulip poplar trees, and spinach plants.

If these plants are exposed to a high level of photochemical oxidants, there may appear small dark dots, larger white spots, and dead areas on the top of the leaf, along with a shiny surface on the bottom of the leaf.

Alfalfa and squash plants are the best indicators of sulfur dioxide pollution in the air. Also, the leaves of cotton, tomato, lettuce, and carrot plants are reliable for monitoring this type of pollution. Among weeds, the widespread ragweed and chickweed plants show damage from sulfur dioxide.

The leaves of these plants are likely to turn yellow if there is a long-term, low-level amount of sulfur dioxide in the air. If they are exposed to a high level of sulfur dioxide, the leaves collapse and become water-soaked.

The air pollution experiments that you can do with plants depend on where you live—what plants grow in your area, and the kinds of air pollution that are found there. In general, plant experiments are best done during the spring and summer. Be sure that the plants you use are healthy to begin with, and not damaged by weather conditions or pests. You may want to set out some potted plants near a power plant, factory, or highway; or you can observe plant life growing near these sources of pollution.

Observing How Air Pollution Affects Clothing

In recent years, stocking manufacturers have received complaints that stockings are not what they used to be. Consumers say that the stockings develop holes without being torn, and wear out much sooner than they did in the past. But scientists are able to show that it is not the stockings that are to blame. It is the pollutants in the air that are ruining many kinds of clothing.

You can show how air pollution affects nylon. Take two clean empty tin cans. Stretch a piece of nylon from an old pair of stockings over the open end of each can. Hold the nylon in place with rubber bands.

Examine the nylon through a magnifying glass. Draw a rough sketch of the arrangement of threads.

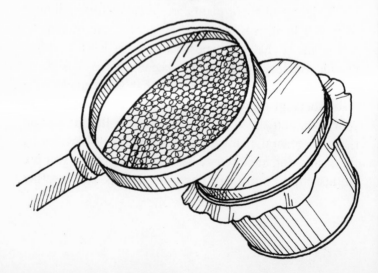

Now place one can upright on a roof, porch, terrace, or similar outdoor place where it will be safe. Avoid placing it near a wall or other obstruction. Keep the other can indoors.

After 30 days, examine both nylon samples through a magnifying glass. Compare the threads in the nylon that was exposed to the air with your sketch. Compare the outdoor sample with the indoor sample. The broken threads in the nylon that was outdoors are caused by the pollutants that are nowadays always present in the air.

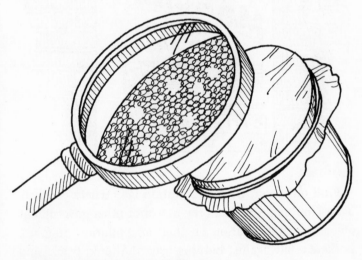

Taking Action Against Pollution

People who are concerned about the effects of air pollution on health and the environment can often accomplish more by joining together than they can alone. Is there a Clean Air Club or other environmental group in your school? If not, why don't you help to start one?

Do you know of any adult groups that are working for clean air in your city or community? Perhaps there are activities in which they would welcome your help.

Find out about the antipollution laws where you live. Your club might write to the mayor or other government officials for information on their air pollution program. Is there a law against burning leaves? Should trucks and cars that emit thick, black smoke be reported to local enforcement agencies? What has been done recently to stop the increase in air pollution?

Learn more about the activities of government and private agencies that work for clean air. Maybe it will be possible for your group to visit their offices or laboratories. Ask for booklets that describe their work.

Here is a list of government agencies and nonprofit public interest groups that are concerned with air pollution:

AIR POLLUTION CONTROL ASSOCIATION
4400 Fifth Avenue
Pittsburgh, Penna. 15213

CONSERVATION FOUNDATION
1717 Massachusetts Avenue NW
Washington, D.C. 20036

ENVIRONMENTAL DEFENSE FUND
162 Old Town Road
East Setauket, N.Y. 11733

ENVIRONMENTAL PROTECTION AGENCY
Office of Public Affairs
Parklawn Building
5600 Fisher's Lane
Rockville, Md. 20852

KEEP AMERICA BEAUTIFUL, INC.
99 Park Avenue
New York, N.Y. 10016

MOBIL OIL CORPORATION
150 East 42 Street
New York, N.Y. 10017

NATIONAL TUBERCULOSIS AND
RESPIRATORY DISEASE ASSOCIATION
1740 Broadway
New York, N.Y. 10019

Look in the telephone book or ask a librarian for the addresses of your state and local pollution control agencies.

Be politically active in the fight for clean air. Urge your parents to vote for candidates who have promised to work for an end to air pollution. Write to your elected legislators and ask them to vote for laws that will control air pollution.

Write articles about air pollution for your school or class newspaper. Run a contest for the best clean-air posters. Post news about progress in air pollution control on school bulletin boards.

Inform your local newspaper, radio station, and television station about your activities; they may want to do a story about you and your group. This publicity will help get others interested in the fight for cleaner air.

The air belongs to all of us. It is our job to help make sure that the air is fit for all living things to breathe.

For Further Reading

BATTAN, LOUIS J. *The Unclean Sky*. Garden City, N.Y.: Doubleday, 1966.

BERGER, MELVIN. *The National Weather Service*. New York: John Day, 1971.

BLUMENSTOCK, DAVID I. *The Ocean of Air*. New Brunswick, N.J.: Rutgers University Press, 1959.

CHANDLER, TONY JOHN. *The Air Around Us*. Garden City, N.Y.: Natural History Press, 1969.

CRAIG, RICHARD A. *The Edge of Space*. Garden City, N.Y.: Doubleday, 1968.

ESPOSITO, JOHN C. *Vanishing Air*. New York: Grossman, 1970.

KAVALER, LUCY. *Dangerous Air*. New York: John Day, 1967.

LAYCOCK, GEORGE. *Air Pollution*. New York: Grosset & Dunlap, 1972.

MARSHALL, JAMES. *The Air We Live in*. New York: Coward-McCann, 1969.

SOOTIN, HARRY. *The Long Search*. New York: Norton, 1967.

Index

ABOUT THE AUTHOR

Melvin Berger's books have introduced young readers to many aspects of science. He has written on *Famous Men of Modern Biology, Tools of Modern Biology,* and *Enzymes in Action.* With the noted cartoonist J. B. Handelsman he has compiled *The Funny Side of Science,* a collection of jokes and cartoons. THE NEW AIR BOOK is a companion volume to *The New Water Book.*

Mr. Berger, a native of New York City, was graduated from the University of Rochester and holds a master's degree from Columbia University. He has also studied at the City College of New York and at London University's Institute of Education. He lives in Great Neck, New York, with his wife, Gilda, who is also a writer, and their two daughters.

ABOUT THE ILLUSTRATOR

Giulio Maestro was born in New York City and studied at the Cooper Union Art School and Pratt Graphics Center. Aside from picture-book illustration, he is well known for his beautiful hand lettering and his book jacket design. He enjoys etching and painting in his free time.

Mr. Maestro lives in Madison, Connecticut.